The Product Diploma

Breaking Into Product Management Out of College

Alan Ni and Davis Treybig

Table of Contents

Introduction

In 2002, the product executive at Google and future Yahoo CEO Marissa Mayer made a big bet. It was the kind of big bet that Google has become known for, but this wasn't a bet on self-driving cars or a game-changing app. It wasn't a bet on the future of Google Maps or Gmail. In fact, the bet wasn't about a product at all - it was about product managers.

Back in the early 2000's product managers were in short supply, or at least the kind that Google was looking for. Google wanted product managers who were deeply technical; people who not only knew how to write code, but who fundamentally understood technology. They also wanted product managers who were hungry and could execute on the smallest details, but who could also think strategically. They weren't finding what they were looking for in the existing pool of product managers.

So Mayer pitched a radical idea: what if Google hired entrepreneurial and talented computer science majors straight out of college and taught them to be product leaders? Google would create a small, close-knit community which could learn the role together as they rotated through different teams in the company. Those in the program would be transformed into the type of product leaders Google wanted - people who could speak in both business and technical terms and who could take products all the way from a high-level idea to a launch. The job would be called Associate Product Manager, or 'APM' for short.

Fast-forward fifteen years and the Google APM program has become one of Mayer's most indelible contributions to the search giant. The first class of Google APMs was just 6 people, but today there is over 40 APMs in each class. Google APMs have gone on to become Google VPs, C-level execs of tech giants like Facebook and Asana, and founders of numerous successful startups such as Optimizely. Former Google CEO Eric Schmidt has said he believes an APM alumni will eventually rise to Google's CEO position.

In fact, Mayer's program was such a success that it has been adopted by almost every other tech giant as well as many successful startups. Today, companies like Facebook, Uber, Dropbox, Workday, and LinkedIn all hire product managers out of college into "APM"-like programs. Although there are some subtle differences between each program - Facebook RPMs (rotational product managers) have 6-month rotations versus Google's year-long rotations, and Microsoft has hundreds of new grad product managers each year - they all have the same foundational goal of finding and developing the product leaders of tomorrow.

In this sense, Mayer created not only a new program at Google, but a entirely new role within the tech industry: the new graduate (or "new grad") product manager. Today, the product manager role has become one of the most coveted and prestigious jobs for ambitious college students, but it is also one of the most competitive and misunderstood. Perhaps you picked up this book because you heard about the product manager role, and want to understand more about what it is and whether it is right for you. Or, perhaps you heard about how rigorous and intimidating the application and interview processes can be, and you want to get a leg up.

We faced those same questions and felt the same way, and that's why we decided to write this book. Before we became Google APMs we were frantically googling: "Should I be a software engineer or PM out of school?", "What do companies look for in new grad PMs?", "How do I prepare for the interviews", and "What does a PM do *exactly*?". At the time, we didn't find great answers and still there aren't many answers out there today.

This book gives you the answers we were looking for; we've synthesized everything we learned through the job search, application, and interview process along with everything we've learned on the job. We discuss what it means to be a product manager and why you could be a good (or bad) fit for the role. We talk about what to do during college, across classes, extracurriculars, and internships, to develop the skills that will help you excel as a PM. Finally, we teach you how to land and then nail a product management interview. For each topic we cover, we've also asked our peers - new grad PMs from Google, Facebook, and other tech companies - to reveal their secrets as well.

By the time you've finished the book, you'll have every piece of information you need to start getting your very own product diploma.

--Davis and Alan

Part 1

Exploring the Field

Ten years ago, only a select few tech giants hired product managers out of college. Today, hundreds of companies do, from real estate startups in Seattle to enterprise software companies in San Francisco. Although the job is more prevalent than ever, it is just as hard as it was 10 years ago for a college student to understand *what exactly a product manager is* and *whether the job is a good fit.*

Like many of you, we had no idea what it meant to be a product manager when we started college. What is the job like? What will I actually do? Will I like it? What can I do after being a PM?

So, before we dive into how to prepare for a PM job when you're in college and land a PM offer, we want to give you some context on the job itself.

If you already know you want to be a product manager, skip to the second section of this book. However, if you're interested in reading first-hand accounts of the day-to-day life of a new grad product manager, hearing from current PMs and APMs about what the job is like, and exploring methods to figure out whether you might be a good fit for a PM role, we encourage you to continue reading.

Plus, the more clearly you understand what the PM role actually is, the better you will be able to prepare for it.

Chapter 1
Being a Product Manager

As a product manager, your role is to create a strategy and plan for what should happen next with your product, align everyone to that plan, and then work with the necessary people to execute on it by building and launching features. This is what has led many, like McKinsey[1], to describe the role as "the mini-CEO of a product". At the end of the day, you are responsible for figuring out the product roadmap and getting the rest of the team on board with that roadmap, and you are responsible for the ultimate success (or failure) of the product.

You will use many skills to achieve your goals as a PM. In order to effectively do your job, you need to be at the center of all of the different functions within your company. For example, you will often need to:

1. Work with engineering and design to scope out and build features to address issues in the product, and move the product in a direction that will ensure success for the company

---

[1] McKinsey, Product Managers for the Digital World, May 2017

2. Work with sales, marketing, account managers, and customer success teams to understand how the product is being received by customers

3. Work with the user research team to see, first hand, how people use your product

4. Work with data analysts to track and measure metrics on things like growth, engagement, and retention

5. Talk to the partnerships teams about potential product integrations with other companies

6. Understand the competitive landscape by studying competing products, and researching trends in the industry

7. Evaluate product risks and tradeoffs with the legal and privacy teams

8. Work with marketing to properly position the product, and to build features that will draw in more potential leads

9. Work with public relations and communications team to manage press cycles and release announcements for your product

This is just a taste - the range of responsibilities you have as a product manager, and the range of people you will work with, is too varied to enumerate. The key point is that you will need to be the person who has **the most context** in your team. You will be a jack-of-all-trades - the person who can make sense of what engineering, design, sales, marketing, legal, finance, biz-dev, strategy, ops, and more are telling you. You will need to aggregate and synthesize that information, evaluating all the pros and cons and tradeoffs, and turn it into an overarching plan that your team can execute on. You will then be in charge of working with engineers, designers, and whoever else is needed to build and launch features according to that plan.

Martin Eriksson, a 20 year expert in the product manager industry, likes to describe the role of a PM with the following diagram[2].

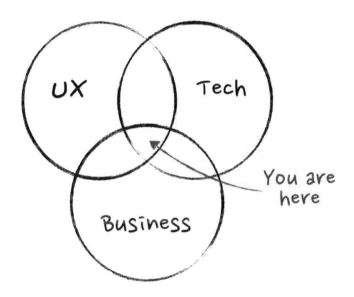

You need to understand the business - what strategy is being set by your CEO or senior executives, what will make the business successful, and how can the product help achieve that.

---

[2] Martin Eriksson, <u>What Exactly is a Product Manager</u>, October 2011

You need to understand user experience - you should be the voice of your users and you need to fight for them. You should know exactly who uses your product, how they use the product, what they love about it, what they hate about it, and how they will react to future changes.

You need to understand technology - at the end of the day, every product decision has engineering implications. A good product manager understands the technical implications of features and works with engineers to evaluate technical tradeoffs.

However, while Martin's diagram does a good job of outlining the key skill sets that are required to be a PM, there is one last thing his diagram doesn't touch on which we think is equally critical in understanding the job of a PM: you need to understand people.

As a product manager, you will need to motivate, inspire, and lead others. You are in the middle of everyone and every team, yet you are not anyone's boss. The engineers don't report to you. The designers don't report to you. **No one reports to you directly.**

So, if you want to be a successful "mini-CEO" of a product, you must learn how to persuade others. You have to come up with a vision that people believe in, and you need to have the ability to pitch and sell that vision.

You'll use data, user research, and user feedback to convince the team why it is worthwhile to build a given feature. You need to be able to explain to the engineers why building feature X will help the sales team close twice as many deals, and to explain to the sales team why building feature Y, which they really want, isn't worthwhile due to the technical tradeoffs.

Ultimately, you need to validate every product decision you make to every stakeholder. Your job is not just to be in the center of business, user experience, and technology, and to create a product roadmap based on that. Your job is to do all that *and to convince the team to follow through on it.*

If you don't successfully align your team, you will struggle in this job, and you will be unable to make progress even if your ideas are good (believe us - we've experienced this!).

However, if you do successfully create a cohesive strategy, you will create a well-oiled machine of different teams all coming together under a single vision, executing on and launching a fantastic product. And you will be in the driver's seat.

—

Product management is a fascinating job that teaches you an immense amount. Because you work with a greater variety of job functions than almost anyone else in the company, you will learn to think in many different ways - like a designer, like an engineer, like a business development person, like a marketer. As a result, every day will be completely different. It's certainly not a monotonous job!

You also develop a lot of leadership characteristics. You will master skills such as coming up with a compelling vision, driving consensus, motivating teams, and conflict resolution.

There's a reason many senior executives and CEOs in the tech industry come from product backgrounds, including Sundar Pichai of Google, Satya Nadella of Microsoft, and Marissa Mayer of Yahoo - the skills you learn as a product manager can be applied almost anywhere.

It's okay if you don't completely understand the job just yet. Because the product manager role is so broad and so based on being the interface between teams (e.g. between design and engineering), it's hard to understand exactly what you will be doing in detail. What matters at this point is that you understand the key, underlying objectives of a product manager. The rest of this chapter will dive into many more details on what being a PM is like.

From the Insiders - Second Year Facebook PM

"I get asked a lot what a product manager does. The short answer is we do whatever is necessary to ship a high-quality product. The longer answer is that it depends on what your team needs. If your team is short on designers, you might have to use Photoshop or Sketch to push your team forward. When you are testing a feature internally and there are issues, you will likely spend a lot of time prioritizing bugs and managing timelines. Once you launch, if you don't have an analyst, you'll need to aggregate the metrics. Basically, you fill in the gaps that your team has, helping wherever you can to ship great products. "

Chapter 2

The Product (Manager) Lifecycle

A good way to understand product management more clearly is to understand the overall lifecycle of products.

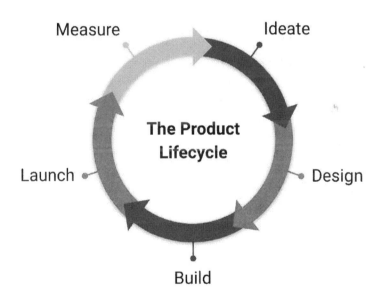

Most products and features go through something close to the above cycle. They begin with **ideation** on the high-level plan for what should be built. Next, the product is **designed** at a high level - what should it look like, what functionality should it support, and how should it be coded. From there, the product is **built**, and as it is built it is tested and the design is iterated on. Finally, you **launch** the product and **measure** how it performs. After that, you analyze what went well and what didn't go well. With what you've learned, you restart the process, ideating again on what should be built next.

Your responsibilities as a product manager will be tied closely to where you are in the product lifecycle:

Lifestyle Stage	PM Responsibilities
Ideation	<ul><li>Competitive Research and Market Analysis</li><li>Foundational User Testing</li><li>Vision Definition and Storytelling</li><li>Consensus Building</li></ul>
Designing	<ul><li>Define success metrics</li><li>Detailed Product Requirements and Mocks</li><li>High Level Technical Design</li><li>Validation of Design with stakeholders</li></ul>
Building	<ul><li>Testing and iterating on the product</li><li>Manage project status and prioritize bugs</li><li>Unblock engineers and find solutions to</li></ul>

	problems that come up • Decide on trade-offs
Launching	• Go-to market strategy with marketing and PR teams • Usability testing • Final approvals and reviews with stakeholders • Internal metrics review • Outreach to customers (e.g. events, blog posts)
Measuring	• Running and resolving a/b tests • Aggregating user feedback • Determining next steps based on data

PM responsibilities broken down by stage of product

In the **ideation** phase, your main goal is to craft a compelling vision for the product and align everyone on it. You will utilize a number of different tools to do this, such as:

1. **Gathering metrics** - how do users use your product today?

2. **User and market research** - analyzing the incentive structures, the players (developers, users, advertisers, etc.), competitors and their different strategies

3. **Leading brainstorming sessions and "sprints"** - meetings where the team all works together to contribute ideas

4. **Project proposals and pitches** - aggregating all the work you've done into some form of presentation or proposal. You'll review this with your team and leadership to ultimately get sign-off to move forward

For instance, let's say you're the PM for the rider experience for Uber, and you're thinking about what your team should prioritize next.

You may start by working with the data analyst team to crunch some numbers about Uber users. Let's say you look into the pick-up experience, and you notice that the average time between when a driver arrives at a pickup location, and when they mark the passenger as picked up, is almost 4 minutes.

This might seem large to you. Why is it taking so long for users to get into a car once it is at their location?

You decide to dig a little bit deeper. You work with the user research team to do a few user studies where you find Uber users and ask them about their most recent pickup experiences. You learn that many of them have trouble finding their driver when he or she arrives, especially because some of the most common pick-up points are crowded areas like restaurants, downtown hubs, and airports.

You follow-up with the data analyst team and validate this assumption - average time between arrival and pickup is *much* higher in residential areas and airports. You know this is an important problem to solve though, because these pickups represent a huge portion of overall pickups.

As a final step to validate your assumption, you run a quick calculation of how much this hurts Uber drivers and users. You find that if you could reduce average arrival-to-pick-up time by 50%, you would increase driver utilization by 10%, which you suspect could increase revenue by at least 2.5%.

You put together a pitch deck and present it to your team. They agree with you that this is an important problem to solve, and so you schedule a review with Uber leadership. You explain the problem, the research you've done, the data you've collected, and some ideas you have about how to solve the issue. You get the OK to move forward.

At this point, you have completed the **ideation** phase. You have a solid idea, and as a good product manager should, you have gotten everyone aligned with your vision. Now, it's time to **design** a solution.

You start by hosting a design sprint with your team, trying to brainstorm as many solutions as possible. What if you had a way for users to give a small note to their driver, describing where they are? What if you sent Bluetooth beacons to drivers, and users could track that beacon on the Uber app to better locate where the driver was? What if users could have a custom image show up in their Uber app that they could hold up to flag down the driver?

Eventually, your team moves from brainstorming to evaluating the ideas mentioned. This idea might be too hard to build. That idea is too complicated for a user. This other idea isn't likely to solve the problem well enough.

You take some of the more promising ideas and turn them into basic prototypes. You go talk to some users about these prototypes. Based on your conversation you have a better sense of what features excite users and where they might get confused or stuck.

Eventually, you might whittle down the list to 2-3 candidate ideas that you think are the most feasible across all dimensions (design, engineering, cost, legal, privacy, and more).

From this point, you will start to work closely with various team members to scope out exactly how these solutions would be built.

You work with designers to build mocks of the end-to-end user flow.

You work with engineers to think through the system design, balancing the product requirements vs. the technical constraints.

You work with data scientists to outline what metrics represent success vs. failure for each idea, and how you would measure those metrics.

Finally, you have reached a point where your ideas are all well defined, and the team is ready to start building and prototyping. You have now reached the **build** phase of product development.

At this point - your job is a lot more about execution and project management. You work with the team to figure out the order of operations for everything. What should be built first? What is our first milestone, and what can come later? How will we test as we build?

Your will be laser-focused on *testing* and *validating* your ideas. You might start by building a very simple prototype of one of your three candidate ideas. It's not working fully and a lot of the functionality is missing, but it is enough for you to test out the experience at a high level.

For instance - you might build a super simple version of a screen in the app that shines a bright color you can hold up while your driver is approaching. You get 15 people on your team to stand on the side of a parking lot with one person as the designated pick-up. Someone else drives up, looking for that pick-up. If the pick-up is holding a particular color that the driver knows about beforehand, does the driver find the pick-up more quickly? Maybe you time this across a few different variations - once with no color, once with only the pick-up shining a color, and once with multiple people having different colors.

If the initial test looks promising, you continue forging ahead as planned. However, more likely than not you'll run into unanticipated problems, both from a design and a technical standpoint. Your job is to continually unblock your team and make sure that they can get over these hurdles with grace. Maybe you pivot to focus on another one of your ideas, you reduce the technical complexity of a feature by cutting one piece of it, or you work with the design team to figure out ways to improve the faults you've noticed during testing.

As the product manager, you are ultimately the one responsible for aggregating all this feedback and data, synthesizing it, and determining what the final product experience should be. You will keep working with your team to test, measure, and iterate until you have a compelling product you believe is ready to officially **launch** (or until you decide that none of the ideas are good, and they should *not* be launched).

In this stage, most of the engineering and design work is done. Your job will shift to working with marketing, public relations, developer-relations, and communications teams. You'll work with them to answer questions like: How should this feature be rolled out? How should it be pitched? When should it be announced?

For instance, let's say the idea mentioned earlier - a colored screen in the app that users can use to flag down their driver - ends up being a good one. For the feature to succeed, you need to get people to use it! So, you might work with the marketing team to draft a blog post about the feature, as well as mentioning it in some upcoming email campaigns.

You might also work with the rider-relations team to attend a few events that Uber hosts for drivers over the following weeks. You'll educate drivers on the new feature, telling them how to use it and how it can help them increase their utilization and make more money.

As the feature starts to roll-out, you will also work with customer support teams, user research teams, and analysts to look at metrics (both qualitative and quantitative) and **measure** success. Are the press and users responding positively? Did you improve the metrics you set out to? Are there any issues people are having which you need to fix?

You'll work with your team to aggregate this information and identify any immediate next steps. For instance, you might need to roll out a few critical bug fixes over the next few days. Or, you may determine that you need change the way that users are introduced to the feature in the app, given that the current opt-in rate is low. You'll ultimately be the one in charge of triaging all this data and feedback, determining the important things to address right away, and the unimportant things that aren't as impactful to fix.

Hopefully, you've done a good job throughout this whole process, and the feature ends up successfully reducing average wait times between driver arrival and customer pickup!

However, your work doesn't stop there. You'll likely take your learnings and use them to identify additional work that could be done in the future. Perhaps you notice that wait times went down at most locations, but not airports, and so you think your team needs to come up with some additional proposals to improve the airport experience. As a result, you're right back at step one, **ideating** a new round of solutions.

—

As you can see, your responsibilities change *drastically* as you drive a feature from inception to launch. You are ultimately the one responsible for creating a great product, and so you will be involved in every step of the way.

You drive the creation of the strategy, you align the team, you work with every different job function to design and build the feature, you coordinate the timeline and milestones, you make sure the feature is tested and well-received, and you drive the launch. You will have help and work with others at every step of the way, but it's your responsibility to make sure everything comes together into a great product launch.

There's one last thing worth mentioning, though. As a Product Manager, you will not just be working on one feature at a time. You might own up to **5-10+ features**, all in different stages of the product lifecycle, at once. This means that on a day to day basis, you are likely doing some combination of *all* of these things.

You'll go from a thirty-minute brainstorming session for feature #1 into a launch meeting for feature #2 into an early user research study for feature #3. You are always utilizing *all* of the skills we mentioned above, from storytelling and pitching, to product design, to analyzing launches.

Now, you should hopefully have a strong sense of what it's like to be a product manager. However, you may be asking, is all of this true even for a product manager right out of college?

Chapter 3

Being a New Grad PM vs. a Senior PM

For the most part, everything we've outlined so far is true for a new grad PM. In our experience, people who join APM or APM-like programs out of college at companies like Google, Facebook, LinkedIn, Asana, and more are given huge amounts of responsibility. That can be a great thing or an overwhelming thing depending on what you're looking for!

A foundational premise of Google's APM program was that APMs would be thrown into the company with the same responsibilities as a more senior product manager and would learn on the job. From what we've heard from APMs in other programs, this is the case for most companies.

While a new grad PM might have a slightly smaller product scope than a senior PM - at the end of the day you are still the product owner, and you have the same responsibilities and functions. The role we have described so far certainly applies to first-year product manager at companies like Google and Facebook.

But, broad descriptions of responsibilities can only explain the job so well. So, let's explore some real examples of "A Day in the Life" of a new grad PM.

From the Insiders - Second Year Google APM

"My first year on the job, I felt like I had most if not all of the responsibilities of a more senior PM. Of course, given it was my first product role, my manager helped me find the right scope to begin with. From there, I grew into owning a larger piece of the product as I was ready. By my second year, my job was virtually indistinguishable from any other PM at the company. Most managers are happy to give you as much responsibility as you can handle."

Chapter 4

A Day in the Life

2nd year Google APM

8:55 - 9:40 AM | Bus to Mountain View from San Francisco

The day starts with me doing a quick scan through my emails and reminders from yesterday. Based on this, I quickly prioritize a list of key tasks I want to get done for the day. I spend the rest of the bus ride responding to my most urgent emails.

9:50 - Noon | Working with engineering and design

When I get into work, I check in with the engineering team on their progress for some of the new features we're building. I discuss bugs with them, helping to prioritize which ones we need to fix vs. which can wait for later (or not be fixed at all).

I also get the opinions of UI/UX designers on some feedback we've been receiving. They mock up some improvements, and we send the mocks to the engineering team to start working on (a "mock" is a sketch/image of how something will look once it is built).

Noon - 12:30 | Lunch

Today I grab lunch with a colleague from my previous team. We discuss our work over some Indian cuisine.

12:30 - 2:30 PM | Marketing

I have a quick meeting with marketing to discuss an upcoming launch that involves external partners. We agree on the next action items during the meeting: crafting a blog post and creating a communications doc for external partners so they can run some marketing campaigns as well.

I spend time after the meeting contributing to and commenting on the blog post, as well as filling in important details for the communications doc.

2:30 - 4:00 PM | Design Meetings

I meet with members from our team as well as other teams to assess the feasibility of a few new features. In one meeting, I present the roadmap for a particular set of features that require API access from another internal team and get their feedback. In another meeting, I talk with our designers to figure out how an existing feature should be modified based on the user feedback.

4:00 - 5:00 PM | VP Review

I spend 30 minutes finishing a deck to present to a vice president at Google. I have these meetings biweekly, and I like to be prepared with metrics and product ideas each time. In the meeting I review some of the experiments that my team ran in the past 2 weeks, as well as some of the launches coming soon. We get a few action items from the VP that I need to follow up on.

5:00 - 6:00 PM | *Gym*

It's hard to find time during the day to work out with a busy PM schedule filled with meetings. To create some space, I block off this one hour chunk in my calendar. Luckily, Google has a gym and shower in my building, so I really have no excuse not to exercise. The physical exertion at the gym is cathartic and helps me relieve stress. After showering and changing, I feel refreshed and ready to close out the day.

6:00 - 7:50 PM | *Ideation and Big Picture Thinking*

The meetings for the day are over so I now have a block of time where I don't have to context switch. This time is super valuable and I use it to think about what to build next and to dive deeper into how our current features are doing. I dig into our analytics dashboard and run some scripts to get the latest engagement data on some new features.

I look for areas where users are dropping off and brainstorm ways to improve engagement for certain features. I share these hypotheses with my engineering and design teams to get their feedback as well. I then synthesize our takeaways into a new feature design doc.

7:50 - 8:40 PM | *Bus home from SF*

After grabbing a to-go dinner (a delicious black bean burger!), I jump on the bus going home. I do a quick pass over my chats and emails to make sure I haven't missed anything urgent that needs to be completed by today. The last thirty minutes of the bus ride, I unplug and read on my kindle (currently working on Being Mortal by Atul Gawande, a great book about the philosophy and ethics of healthcare).

1st year Google APM

8:30 - 9:00 AM | Breakfast

I start my day by getting to work and eating breakfast at one of Google's cafes. As I eat my eggs, toast, and coffee, I read through my daily list of tech industry newsletters.

9:00 - 9:30 AM | Email and Plan Day

After breakfast, I catch up on my emails from the night before, skimming through a bunch and then focusing on four that require more in-depth responses.

My first email involves giving my opinion on how to approach a product decision that needs to be made based on an engineering tradeoff. I outline some pros and cons and from there propose a solution.

In another email I give our UX researcher some of my thoughts about an upcoming user study we are planning.

In my third email I give some further context to one of the tech leads I work with, who had some feedback about a feature I proposed the prior week.

Finally, I answer some clarifying questions from one of the engineers I work with.

9:30 - 10:00 AM | UX Meeting

Next, I go to my first meeting of the day with a designer on my team. We go over some mocks he has made for an upcoming feature and talk through some open questions. I provide some feedback on areas where there is a disconnect between some engineering decisions and the mocks, and then we debate a few other design questions. We end the meeting by deciding that we probably need one more round of iteration before we can get started building the feature.

10:30 - 11:00 AM | Weekly Sync

After my UX meeting, I head to a weekly meeting for one of the major features I am working on. Engineering work is now heavily underway, so this is mainly an opportunity for me to make sure nothing is blocking the engineers.

We do a quick sync on status, and then I clarify whether they think we are still on track to hit a few of our milestones over the next few weeks. We discuss one lingering engineering decision that needs to be made, evaluating the pros and cons of each choice we have and then making a call.

Finally, they point out that they are worried about another team that has not made much progress on an API which needs to be built for this feature to work. I say that I will track this down, and I schedule a meeting with myself, one of our engineers, and this other team the next day to talk about this issue.

11:00 AM - 12:00 PM | PRD

After my morning meetings, I dedicate an hour to working on a "PRD", or product requirements doc, for a feature I want the team to focus on next quarter.

Although I think I have a strong high level idea of what needs to be built, a lot of the subtler details still need to be ironed out. What will this look like? Should we focus on this type of user or that type of user? What metrics should we track to analyze the feature? How should we prioritize the different sub-features?

I spend about 45 minutes trying to answer these questions, at which point I realize I need some broader feedback on some of them. I decide to schedule a meeting with my manager to talk through my ideas, so I spend the last 15 minutes writing down the key questions I want to ask him.

12:00 - 12:30 PM | Lunch

I head to one of Google's numerous lunch spots to have lunch with a friend of mine, and we talk about random things unrelated to work for thirty minutes.

12:30 - 1:00 PM | Privacy Review

After lunch, I meet with someone in Google's privacy team to talk through the privacy implications of a feature I am working on. We walk through the data collection that the feature would require, and she voices one concern. I propose a few different ways we could try to alleviate that concern, such as by reducing the scope of what we log, and we ultimately come to a conclusion.

Since we finish talking early, I file a bug to one of my engineers to track this change before heading to my next meeting.

1:00 - 2:00 PM | Weekly Product Meeting

I arrive at my team's weekly product meeting, where typically 1-2 people present what they are working on for the rest of the team to offer feedback. I am not presenting anything today, so I just sit back and listen to some of my co-workers outline their product proposals.

In the second presentation, I realize there is an opportunity for a better integration between one of my features and something that this PM is working on. I make a note to email them some ideas later.

2:00 - 2:30 PM | Meeting with Marketing

I have a launch coming up for one of my features, so I scheduled a meeting with marketing to discuss whether this feature warrants being included in any blog posts or other marketing medium.

I explain the feature, its potential impact and who I think it would be most useful for, and my coworker from the marketing team asks a few clarifying questions. We end up deciding that this feature may fit inside another blog post they were planning to do in a few weeks, and so he tells me that he will send me the draft once it is ready for me to add some content.

2:30 - 3:30 PM | Email

After my afternoon string of meetings, I head back to my desk and spend about an hour managing my inbox.

- I read through a design document sent out by one of the engineers I work with and add some comments

- I read through a PRD sent by another PM and add some comments

- I send out notes from my meetings today, recapping key action items and follow ups

- I send an email to the PM who presented in the weekly meeting earlier

- I read through a lot of other emails that require no immediate action on my part

- I quickly glance at a few changelists submitted for review, and make sure the sample screenshots look as expected. I add 1-2 comments to one of the changelists saying that the UI doesn't match the designer's mocks

3:30 - 4:00 PM | Design Kickoff for New Feature

Next, I head to a meeting with the designers and researchers I work with regularly to outline a new feature I want us to build soon. The goal here is to talk through the high level goals of the feature and identify what needs to be done on the design side of things. Do we need to do a user study? When should we plan on doing mocks and prototypes?

We decide that the feature is simple enough to not require any studies, and determine that we will work on designs for this after the designer finishes up their current task in the next week or two.

4:30 to 5:30 PM | User Study Observation

Finally, I end my day by observing a user study run by one of our UX researchers for another feature I work on. This is a usability study, so we are having users interact with a prototype and give us feedback. I take notes on the areas of the product where the candidate has difficulties, and mark down some key things to think through and potentially change.

At the end of the study, I quickly sync with the other observers to compare thoughts.

Rest of the day

I go home after 5:30, hit the gym, and then grab dinner at Chipotle. I then return home, shower, and wind down with an episode of Narcos on Netflix.

At around 10:00 PM I quickly check my email for just 10 minutes before I go to bed and respond to one semi-urgent email. I read for a little bit, and finally go to bed around 10:45 PM.

2nd year Facebook RPM

8:30 to 9:30 AM | Review for Exec Presentation

I'm the PM of a major new feature we're trying to launch. Because this feature is really important strategically, I lead bi-weekly executive reviews on the vision and status.

I spend the morning refining the slide deck I have prepared for the meeting, which outlines some key product decisions, UI mocks, and engineering status updates. I also spend some time practicing the presentation.

9:30 AM - 10:30 AM | UX Research Report

We recently ran a large UX study to get feedback on some product ideas the team has. The researchers are presenting out their final report from the study. The presentation lasts about 30 minutes, after which we have some follow up discussions about the implications of the report. We agree on some key principles to adhere to as we move forward with these ideas.

10:30 AM - 11:00 AM | Exec Review

I have my exec review and it generally goes well. We spend a significant amount of time discussing one product decision, and end up deciding we should go a different direction. As I leave the meeting, I begin to compile all of the things that will need to change to support this new product direction.

11:00 AM - 1:00 PM | Emails and Follow ups

I spent the next two hours triaging emails and sending follow-ups from meetings this morning. I also start to scope out an outline of how to approach the feature the exec team asked us to change, and send it over to my engineering team and designers for feedback.

1:00 PM - 2:00 PM | Lunch

2:00 PM - 3:00 PM | Data Analysis

We recently launched an experiment to measure a change we implemented. Since my team doesn't have a dedicated data analyst, I do some SQL queries to quantify the impact of the feature.

I compile the results in a small deck and share it with my team. It looks like the feature did what we expected it to do!

3:00 PM - 3:30 PM | Engineering Sync

Next up is a weekly status meeting for one of the teams I work with. We go through issues the engineering team faced in the past week and discuss ways to resolve them. We also decide we need to get more user feedback on something we're working on, and I tell the team I will follow up with our user researchers.

3:30 PM - 5:30 PM | Work Time

I'm done with meetings for the day, so I spend the rest of my afternoon working on some planning for the next quarter. I have a couple ideas for next steps we should be taking with the product, so I start to put together a pitch deck.

I end the day by marking down other things I need to follow up on tomorrow.

1st Year Linkedin APM

7:30- 9:00 AM | Morning Routine, Gym, Drive to Work

I start the day with my morning routine: making my bed, a few minutes of silent meditation, and assembling my gym gear. Next, I head over to the gym where I turn off notifications, listen to music, and power through a workout. Afterwards, I head to LinkedIn HQ, use the showering facility on my floor, change into my work attire, and walk to my desk.

9:00 - 9:30 AM | Email and Task Management

At my desk, I start by checking Todoist (a task management system), where I take a glance at my work related tasks for the day. Once I have an idea of the most important things I want to tackle, I quickly glance at my calendar to review my schedule for the day.

I have a bit of time before my first meeting, so I catch up on a few key work emails, and then read some of the daily newsletters I'm subscribed to, including Data Sheet by Fortune Magazine, the Morning Brew, The Download by MIT Tech Review, and Stratechery.

9:30 - 10:00 AM | Engineering Stand-up

My first meeting of the day is an engineering stand up (a meeting where we all just stand and talk rather than go to a conference room) for a feature we're hoping to launch soon. At LinkedIn, we work in two week sprints and have a few check-ins sprinkled throughout those two weeks to make sure the team is on track the complete the agreed upon tasks. If there are any obstacles or roadblocks that come up, my job is to determine the best point of contact to resolve them so the team can keep making progress.

10:00 - 11:00 AM | Product Marketing Meeting

I then head to my next meeting - a conference call with a product marketing manager (PMM) I work with regularly. This week we're discussing the marketing narrative for one feature I'm building. She asks a few questions about how to position the feature for various use cases, and we brainstorm a few ideas and discuss the pros and cons of each. We end the meeting with a baseline proposal, and a few follow-ups I need to address with my team.

11:00 - 11:30 AM | LinkedIn Lunch

Today, I grab a quick lunch with a friend on my team.

11:30 AM - 12:00 PM | Emails

After lunch, I spend some time clearing out my inbox. I decide which emails I can archive, which ones to address later and respond to the emails that need immediate attention.

12:00 - 2:30 PM | Time Block for Work

I purposefully set aside regular time for deeper work that requires longer bouts of focus, such as writing out a product spec or making a roadmap deck. It's vital to carve out time to think and work on tasks without being interrupted by meetings.

During this specific work block, I start a draft of a deck which outlines an early vision for a feature I want to work on in the coming months. I asses some of the key strategic questions which I need to solve, such as the specific type of user to target, the goals and non-goals of the feature, and its positioning to end-users. I end this work block by identifying some clear next steps to make further progress, such as a few other teams I should follow up with and get feedback from.

2:30 - 3:00 PM | Growth Tiger Team Meeting

I spend part of my time as a "growth" PM, working alongside people in business operations, marketing, engineering and design to rapidly test small changes to user onboarding flows with experiments. The ultimate goal here is to improve our user acquisition funnel, and help LinkedIn grow more quickly.

I help to manage and prioritize the list of hypotheses we want to test, working with all the stakeholders in this mini-growth team to brainstorm and then plan experiments.

This week, we work on a plan for a redesign of one of our landing pages. We discuss some UX options, the metrics we want to track, and our release plan and timeline.

3:00 - 4:00 PM | Weekly Product Leads Meeting

During this meeting, the head of product for my org at LinkedIn sits down with all of the product managers, the head of design, and the head of business operations to share major updates, such as strategic plans, upcoming events and launches, and cross-org news.

Today, he touches on some of our key priorities for the upcoming year. Afterwards, we have a discussion where we ask follow-up questions about how those priorities relate to each of our areas.

4:30 to 5:30 PM | Design Meeting

Two designers and I meet for an hour to discuss a recent user study we ran for an upcoming feature. During this study, we showed users a few mock-ups of this feature and how it would work, and then probed them with questions about what they thought. We are now going through all of our notes from those sessions, highlighting key takeaways and areas where the product was not received by users as we intended.

We notice a few aspects of the feature which could clearly be improved upon based on the user feedback, and end the meeting with a list of next steps for me to follow-up on with the engineering team.

Rest of the day

Depending on the day, my post-work routine varies from playing on the LinkedIn basketball team at the Bay Club to attending meditation and yoga classes to just catching up with friends.

Today, I just head back home, call my parents and talk to them for a bit, and then practice music for a while (piano, learning the guitar, and singing) before reading for 30 minutes and then going to bed.

Chapter 5

Identifying whether Product Management is Right for You

You now understand the high-level job description of a product manager, and have also seen some examples of what your day-to-day life might be like. You have a solid grasp on the fact that it will be your job to gather data from as many contexts as possible, to use that data to identify what should be built next, and to work with designers and engineers to build it. You are probably even excited at the prospect of being a "Mini-CEO".

But, it's worth taking the time to consider what makes someone a good fit for product management. The job is not right for everyone, and some personalities will likely not enjoy working as a product manager.

You may enjoy product management if:

1. **You enjoy multitasking** and thinking about problems in many different ways (marketing, sales, policy, privacy, legal, design, engineering, partnerships, etc.)

2. **You enjoy working with people**. As a PM, you will have to meet with people a lot. You will have to present to large groups. You will lead virtually every meeting you are a part of. And, a

huge part of your job will be to persuade and motivate people to get them on board with your vision. You will have to manage disagreements between teams and figure out how to align them. Some degree of extroversion is likely valuable (though not required).

3. **Higher level strategic questions interest you.** You like to think about strategy and high level product direction just as much as you enjoy thinking about detailed technical problems.

4. **You are okay with not being a direct "builder".** You will define the product direction, but at the end of the day it's the engineers who write the code, the designers who make the mocks, and the business development and sales teams that close the deals. We cannot stress how important this is - as a PM you may feel as close to the implementation level because you can't really get your hands dirty and build something yourself. You have to get others to do so (and you're not their manager, so you better be good at persuasion and selling yourself).

5. **You are strongly self-motivated.** As a PM, there will be no one telling you what to do. Even as a new grad, you will come in and own a certain area of the product. It's on you to figure out what to do and how to make it happen.

6. **You like to "corral the herd" and can chase things down aggressively.** Most PMs we know are somewhat "type A" in this sense. When a critical launch date is nearing, or when a major problem occurs that needs to be fixed ASAP, or when a sudden

disagreement puts the product roadmap at risk, you will need to chase down the relevant stakeholders and fix the problem.

You should be wary of Product Management if:

1. **You like to dig in deep to really complex technical problems and solve them**. While as a PM you will work closely with engineers, it is ultimately not your job to solve the really challenging technical problems that many engineers relish. You won't have times where you are spending 3-4 hours focused on a single problem. Your work will be wide, but shallow.

2. **You want to feel like you are directly building things**. If you like to directly create, you may be better off working as an engineer. Product Management is ultimately a "hands off" role in terms of creating things.

3. **You don't want to deal with constant context switching**. If you don't like constant meetings and regular interruptions, don't like having to juggle 5 different teams building 5 different features at once, or don't want to go from thinking about an engineering constraint to a marketing pitch to a design session within a 1 hour timespan, this job probably isn't for you.

4. **You dislike dealing with people or public speaking**. Being a good people manager is critical to being a good PM. You will have to navigate the organization to get an array of stakeholders on board, and you will have to think about the motivations and interests of each party to learn how to work with them. If you

aren't interested in learning how to persuade others, we doubt that you'll enjoy being a PM.

5. **You like to be able to directly quantify what you have done or directly measure your output.** On a day to day basis, it is very hard to define whether or not you made progress as a PM. Maybe you ran a meeting, or sent some emails, but did that have impact? You won't know until much later, when the overall product finally launches. This differs completely from being a software engineer or data analyst, where you can generally quantify *exactly* what you've done on a given day.

6. **You hate meetings**. As a product manager, you are the interface between all the different teams and stakeholders involved in a product. So, you will have a *lot* of meetings. If you don't like meetings, do not take this job!

We know several people who have joined new grad PM programs and quit within a year because the job was a poor fit. Some preferred the simplicity of getting to focus on engineering challenges without interruptions. Others disliked the "bullshit" or "political" work of having to motivate and persuade people, align teams, and drive consensus. Others weren't fulfilled because they were too distanced from directly producing output (e.g. code or mocks); they felt like they weren't contributing, even if they were.

Take a second and introspect. It's essential you are excited about **all** aspects of the job, not just the product strategy and brainstorming aspects. You will have to drive consensus, you will have to chase down bugs before before a launch and manage the hell out of the different teams to hit your launch target, you will have to switch between 5-10 different topics a day, and you will probably have days with nonstop, back-to-back meetings for 4+ hours straight.

For the right kind of person, these tasks can be incredibly rewarding and fun. It's exhilarating to hit a launch when you were right up against the wire. It's also incredibly rewarding to become good at persuading and "selling" people on your vision. Plus, you will learn so much about so many different topics because of how multidisciplinary the role is.

But, for the wrong person, the job won't feel right. We hope that we have given you a good framework to figure out which camp you fall into. If you're still unsure, we recommend reaching out to some current PMs at companies you are interested in and chatting with them about what they like and don't like about their job. The more people you talk to, you will gain a better sense of whether this is the right job for you.

From the Insiders - Google Software Engineer

"After doing multiple internships as a PM and software engineer, I realized that what I liked most was to be hyper-focused on a single problem. While getting to wear many hats at once was fun for me at times, at other times it felt like I could never get into a flow state. In the end, I decided I enjoyed the depth of software engineering more than the breadth of product management and decided to start my career as a software engineer."

Chapter 6

Product Management vs. Other Jobs

In our experience, most of the people looking at product management roles out of college are also considering at least one or two other types of jobs. So, let's dive into how to compare product management to the most common alternative jobs new grad PM candidates tend to look at.

Software Engineering vs PM

By far, the most common career dilemma for new grad PMs is working in software engineering versus product management. In some respects, these roles are similar. Both are fairly technical and involve computer science focused problems, both will result in you working in the tech industry, both will be compensated similarly, and both have great opportunities for career development.

So, how do you decide? The fundamental difference between the two roles is breadth vs. depth.

As a software engineer, your primary role is to dive very deep into a specific feature or problem. You will work with your PMs and tech leads on a small set of features that need to be built, and you will be in charge of every aspect of *how* they are built - what system design, what infrastructure, what algorithms, what components, etc. You will need to be a technical expert, mastering a specific way of thinking to address these questions.

As a product manager, your primary job is to go broad, driving the strategy for a large area of the product. You will be involved in an array of features and initiatives, but you will only define their requirements at a high level. You will need to be a jack-of-all-trades and adopt a multi-faceted mindset, but you will never be the expert on any given area.

As a software engineer, you will work on a given problem for weeks or months, starting with a high level design document and moving through coding the logic, writing the tests, and debugging and fixing issues that arise.

As a product manager, you will work on problems in chunks of 30 minutes to one hour, constantly switching each day between the 10-20 different things you may be working on.

As a software engineer, you will primarily work alone as you write code. When interacting with others, it will primarily be other software engineers on your immediate team, and each of you will be thinking about problems in similar ways.

As a product manager, you will virtually always be working with other people, and in each interaction you will be shifting your thinking style based on who you are talking to (whether that be designers, engineers, marketing, or sales).

As you can see, this breadth vs. depth difference manifests in many ways. Software engineers focus on *fewer* problems, analyze those problems at a much *deeper* level for a *longer* period of time, and are consistently applying the same *technical* mindset. Product managers focus on a *wide number* of problems and analyze them *in a shallower but more multidisciplinary way.*

So, think about what resonates more with you. For many people, being a software engineer will be preferable to being a PM. While a software engineer doesn't get to wear as many hats, work at as high a level strategically, or interact with as many people, they also don't have to constantly multitask, fill their days with meetings, or spend so much time trying to influence or persuade others across the company. Going broad has its downsides, and for many people, it isn't worth it.

A software engineer gets to focus on building things, writing code, and solving really interesting technical problems. Believe us, as a PM, you'll sometimes wish you could simplify your life and do just that.

But, if the breadth and multifaceted nature of product management appeals to you, then you may want to try it out!

Is it better to be a SWE first if I want to be a PM in the long run? Will being a SWE help prepare me more for being a PM?

In our experience, if you have a computer science or computer engineering major, you definitely have a strong enough technical background to be a great PM.

In this case, working as a software engineer will likely add little incremental value. You are much better off becoming a PM as soon as possible, and directly developing the full PM skill set on the job.

If you compare the skills, ability, and seniority of someone who works as a software engineer for 4 years, then becomes a PM for 2, vs. someone who works as a PM for 6 years, the person who started as a PM out of college will be ahead in every way.

We meet a lot of people who ask if it is strategic to do software engineering just to become a PM. Being a software engineer certainly does not hurt your ability to eventually be a PM, and many people transfer from software engineering to product. However, transferring is not trivial - at a lot of companies it involves getting a sponsor, convincing someone to let you do product work, and doing that for a few months until you get the opportunity to interview. Then, you have to go through a set of interviews, and you may or may not get approved to transfer. Furthermore, if you do get approved, you'll typically be down leveled. So, if you were a "level 5" software engineer, you'll become a "level 4" product manager.

Do not put yourself through this trouble if you know you want to be a PM. Put in the work to become a PM straight out of college, and you'll be able to do what you want earlier and get better at it more quickly.

Is Product Management "better" than software engineering?

Product management is sometimes glamorized as a post-college role, which is likely due to the fact that the ratio of PMs to engineers is very low, and thus PM roles seem more exclusive. We feel that sometimes people choose product management over software engineering just because of that exclusivity and rareness, rather than because the job is truly a good fit.

Don't fall for this - the roles are very different, and one is not better than another. Career opportunities, career progression, and compensation won't heavily differ between the two, so pick based on the skillset you will enjoy developing. For a lot of people, engineering might be a better choice.

Consulting vs PM

On the other end of the spectrum are candidates who are considering management consulting at companies like McKinsey, Bain, and BCG versus product management. There is a much greater difference between consulting and product management than there is between software engineering and product management, so tread carefully if this a decision you are making.

First, consider the industry. In consulting, you can (and probably will) work on a variety of different cases in very different industries: consumer packaged goods, retail, manufacturing, airlines, tech, finance, etc. This is really exciting in some respects - you learn a lot about a wide range of businesses. On the other hand, it can be non-ideal. Sometimes, you will be assigned a case that you truly don't care about, like optimizing manufacturing efficiency for widget #2, or organization optimization (aka firing people). If you are excited about the innovation happening in the tech industry like we are, you are almost certainly better off just working in the tech industry (and no, working in McKinsey's digital division is not the same).

Second, consider working as an operator versus in the services industry. As a consultant, you are given a problem, your team works to analyze data to propose a solution, and then for the most part you leave. Your deliverable is a plan, not necessarily a realized result. On the other hand, as a product manager, your job is truly end to end. You do the planning *and* the implementation. As a result, you will see much less variety than a consultant who can typically work on something new every 2-3 months, but you learn what it takes to actually execute.

Third, consider work/life balance. As a consultant you have to travel a lot and you will generally work longer hours. Since you are in client services, you need to do everything you can to please your client, and sometimes that means having to pull an all-nighter or totally re-do a proposal because your client suddenly decided they didn't like something.

Finally, consider the work itself. As a consultant, your primary tasks will be:

1. Researching a company and its industry by reading a lot and talking to experts

2. Analyzing data in excel

3. Conducting interviews with employees in the company and others who interface with the company (e.g. its customers, its partners)

4. Making powerpoint decks

5. Selling or pitching to clients

You will become really good at excel, presenting and sales, and learning how to work with clients.

In contrast, as a PM, your tasks are much more varied. While you won't be presenting to CEOs of companies all the time, you will be interacting with engineers, designers, user researchers, marketers, lawyers, and more every day. You will learn how to execute and manage deadlines and handle launches. You will get to think both strategically and get detailed. Your work will be more varied than being 80% focused on excel and powerpoint, but it will still be analytical - every product decision you make at companies like Google and Facebook will be data driven (and you will use data analysis tools more complex than excel). While you won't be selling to a client, you will be selling to your teammates and your directors every day as a PM as you try to sell your roadmap.

So, if you're excited about getting to explore a number of really different industries and bounce between them every few months, and you are happy to focus on strategy, not execution, then being a management consultant may be for you.

But if you want a better work life balance, you know you want to work in the tech industry, and you want to learn a broader variety of skills and actually build things, we would recommend trying to be a product manager. One of us was seriously considering an offer from McKinsey out of college, but it was these factors that led to choosing Google instead. It was absolutely the right decision, especially given what we have seen from our friends who went into consulting, and are now overwhelmingly trying to leave and break into tech product management.

> ### *From the Insiders - First Year Workday PM*
>
> "When I was graduating I was lucky enough to have the opportunity to choose between consulting and PM roles. I really liked the people I talked to in both roles and the exposure the roles would provide me. I ended up choosing a PM role because I knew that long-term I wanted to work in the technology space. Given that, product management was clearly the better choice. "

Startup vs. PM

A final common consideration among potential new grad product managers is whether they should be an APM at a big company or join a startup.

We think this mostly boils down to the following criteria:

1. **Risk**: Joining a small company is definitely far riskier in terms of job security and career development. Most startups fail, whereas you can continually become more senior year over year at a place like Facebook or Twitter. (Don't be overconfident in your ability

to pick startups - even the best venture capitalists in the world only make money back on 10-30% of their investments)

2. **Compensation**: Although you can make a ton of money at a startup if it does really well and IPOs, your risk adjusted compensation will be much higher at a larger company.

3. **Work-life balance**: You will likely work far more hours at an early stage startup.

4. **Variety of work**: Regardless of your official job title, at a startup you need to be willing to do everything. You may help with customer support. You may help with recruiting and HR. Your scope of work will be much broader.

5. **Learning potential**: Your pace of learning at a startup will likely be higher than in a large company because of how much there is to do. You may not know how to run online marketing, but you may be the only person with time to do it. So, you have to figure it out.

6. **Excitement and growth**: Startups feel very different to work in - there is an excitement and energy associated with the high risk, high reward nature of startups. Being part of a "rocketship" company which is growing like crazy is a truly unique experience that can't really be matched by working at a Google or Facebook.

If you talk to different people or read advice from different leaders in the tech industry, you will hear very different opinions about this question.

Some people think you are better off joining a big company for at least a few years at first. This helps you hedge against risk. If you ever join a startup that fails, if you have a great experience like being an APM at LinkedIn on your resume, it won't be hard to find another job at a great company very quickly. This is particularly true if you're interested in product management, since it is almost impossible to join an early stage startup as a PM. At that stage, the CEO typically fulfills the responsibilities of a PM. If they are going to hire anyone in product management at that stage, it is going to be someone with a lot of experience, as they can't afford to teach or grow a new PM like a larger company can.

Others will say that while you are young and fresh out of college, you have a greater ability to take risks than at any other point in your life. You likely have no kids, no spouse, and no major financial commitments, and so it is the perfect time to join an early stage startup. If it does well, you will not only make a huge amount of money, but you will have likely learned far more, and grown into a role of far greater responsibility, than you would have at a more established company. If it doesn't do well, then you can still hustle and get a good job at another place.

Ultimately, you can make an argument either way, and the choice is a personal one. That said, if you're not sure of a company's trajectory, in general, there is a lot to gain from an APM-like program at Google or Facebook (though we may be a *bit* biased). Working at a larger company will give you the context and training you need to work as a product manager, and is a very small time commitment relative to the degree it helps you hedge against future potential failed startups. After one or two years, if the entrepreneurial bug is still biting you, go join a startup as a PM thanks to your training at the larger company.

From the Insiders - Current Startup PM, Former Google APM

"When I was leaving college, I had a tough decision to make between joining a startup I interned for and going into a product role. Even though I knew I eventually wanted to join a smaller company, I decided to join Google because I wanted to learn about product management in a more structured environment. I don't regret my decision and I think that it would've been really tough to get the mentorship I received at Google at a startup."

Next Steps

We've now walked you through just about every aspect of being a PM out of college. We've explained the job itself, we've shared detailed examples of a day in the life of a PM, we've outlined the personality traits that make good product managers, and we've compared the PM job to the other jobs which you might be considering.

Our goal so far has been to give you an excellent sense of whether you're interested in being a product manager or not. For those of you who are, keep reading, as the rest of this book will now focus on helping you become a product manager.

The second section of this book, **"Preparing for the Job"**, will describe how to prepare for a product management job in college. We'll describe what classes to take, what extracurriculars to focus on, and what skills you need to learn.

The final section, **"Getting the Job"**, will outline how to prepare your resume, what companies to apply to, the application process, the interview process, and how to evaluate offers.

Being a product manager is truly an amazing job. It's fun, it's dynamic, you get huge amounts of responsibility, and you learn so much. We hope that you're as excited as we were to become product managers, and we can't wait to walk you through exactly what you need to do to land a job in product management out of college.

Part 2

Preparing for the Job

So you know that you want to be a PM out of college. The next question is - how do you do it? Are there specific classes you should take? What side projects should you focus on? And what internships do you need to land?

This chapter of the book will touch on all of these questions. If you're already a senior, and you're just looking for advice on applying to and landing a product management job, then skip to the third chapter. But, if you still have some time left in college, you can use these tips to maximize your chances both of landing a PM job, and of doing well in it.

We'll start by reviewing the key skills you need to develop to become an effective product manager (and therefore to get recruiters' attention). From there, we'll jump into specific advice on classes, internships, and much more.

Chapter 7

Key skills to develop in college

We recommend that you focus first and foremost on **skills** rather than specific activities, side projects, or classes.

We all have different interests and passions. We want you to become a PM while being true to those passions. Not only will you be much happier doing this, but you will shine much more as an applicant by presenting a unique story, rather than having the exact same resume as hundreds of other applicants.

Furthermore, not every activity or class is available to every person. For instance - not every college has hackathons. So, it wouldn't make sense for us to just tell you to do hackathons to demonstrate technical prowess.

We would rather teach you the skills you need to demonstrate when applying to PM roles, and leave it to you to figure out the right set of opportunities to develop those skills.

So, what are the key skills you should be focusing on? Well, they are same core skills you need in your day to day life as a Product Manager - **leadership, communication, product strategy and design,**

analytical thinking, and technical skills. We'll go through these one at a time.

Leadership

If nothing else, a product manager needs to be a leader. If you can come up with a compelling vision and inspire the people around you to drive that vision forward, you will likely be a very effective PM.

Steve Jobs was famously described as having a "reality distortion field". He was so adept at persuading those around him into believing in an idea, no matter how ambitious, that they would almost ignore reality to try and see it through. Jobs achieved this with a combination of charisma, enthusiasm, storytelling, and an understanding of people (both users and his co-workers).

These are critical skills to master as a product manager. **The best way to develop them is to take on opportunities where you are managing, leading, or otherwise working with a group**. This might mean taking classes which involve many group projects. It might mean joining a club where you work with others towards some goal. It may even mean working on a side project with some friends.

In these situations, strive to be the person who takes initiative and drives the team forward. Set-up and run the meetings. Define the milestones. Pitch the group on your ideas. Figure out how to align everyone and get them on the same page. Take it on yourself to resolve disagreements and figure out how to make each member of your team effective.

As an example, we've all heard the story of the person who gets put in some group in college that is terrible. Maybe one person never shows up to meetings. Another person is not following the plan at all. Two others are constantly fighting. **If you get put into a situation like this, figure out how to lead the group and make it functional.**

This may involve doing things like:

1. Taking ownership of all planning and organization.

2. Delegating tasks in a way that maximizes the chance that each person will be successful

3. Working to resolve disagreements or interpersonal conflict

4. Doing the tasks that no one else will do, but are critical to the group's success

By putting yourself in situations like this, you will start to get better at inspiring and leading others. You will also get some excellent stories of times you succeeded at leading a team, or failed but learned something in the process. These experiences will be invaluable for your resume, for your interviews, and for your eventual work as a PM.

Communication

Very closely related to leadership is communication - can you communicate clearly via both writing and speaking? Note that we are using communication as a broad term that comprises many sub-skills:

1. **Presentation and public speaking** - Can you get in front of a group and present an argument?

2. **Listening** - Are you good at *listening to and understanding* other people? This is a central to being a great communicator.

3. **Having difficult conversations** - Can you talk through challenging situations with people? Can you handle these situations with tact and grace?

4. **Storytelling** - Can you take any topic and make it captivating?

These are all *essential* attributes to being an effective PM.

You will lead virtually every meeting you are part of and will regularly have to present to your team and to your company's leadership.

You will need to listen to all of your stakeholders (engineers, designers, marketing, sales, customer support, etc) to understand the problems they face and how certain product decisions will affect them.

You will have to have navigate complicated inter-team dynamics. There will be times when people or teams are upset or angry and you will need to figure out how to resolve that to push the product forwards.

You will have to take user feedback, data, competitive research, and more, and turn it into a compelling story that people can buy into.

To develop these skills, you should seek out two main kinds of scenarios. First, find situations where you are pitching or presenting to others, preferably large groups of people. This might be a finance club where you pitch a new stock each week, it might be a class on public speaking, or it may be a sales internship one summer.

Second, find situations where you have to work with others (similar to the situations where you develop leadership skills). This is where you need to practice listening to others, understanding their motivations, and handling tough interpersonal situations.

Your end goal should be that you are superb at communicating with people in all situations, from one on one to very large crowds. Figure out what you can do to demonstrate this skill to recruiters and interviewers.

Product Strategy and Design

While being a leader and communicating well are critical to being an effective PM, you also need to be good at product thinking. What do we mean by this? You should be able to effortlessly talk about any product (technical or non-technical) from a very high level all the way down to the smallest detail.

At the highest level, you need to understand product strategy. Why is a product built the way it is? Why is it oriented around a certain type of customer? What need does this product fulfill? What is the business model? How do the competitive landscape and the players in the market influence the product?

At the lowest level, you need to be able to talk through detailed aspects of product design. Why does this screen look like this? Which user flows are done well, and which are done poorly? If you were building feature X, what would it look like? Could you walk me through the end-to-end user experience?

There are many ways to develop these skills. For product strategy, you might start by staying up to date on magazines, websites, newsletters, books, or other material that touches on business strategy. Read Forbes, The Economist, Fortune, TechCrunch, or the Wall Street Journal. When you see articles about products or companies and *why they are doing what they do*, critically analyze them. Do you agree with the argument laid out? What evidence might lead to a contrary opinion?

An even better way to develop strategic product thinking is to engage in activities that involve you actively coming up with your own theses on business. This could be a case competition or an economics class where you write papers on incentive structures. Or, just find a friend and commit to each writing a short one page analysis of an app you like. Then, talk through your ideas together. What matters is that you get in the habit of critically analyzing complex businesses and products.

For product design, try to do something that involves building products at a more detailed level. Build some simple websites as a side project. Do design work for clubs at your school. Or, publish some analyses of products you use a lot - what are user needs they fail to meet, what are workflows that could be improved, and what is designed well?

You can also explore reading books about design, or following popular designers or product leaders who write about design. Listen to how they talk about design problems - you want to learn how to think like a designer. That involves getting good at things like:

1. Clearly describing goals and non-goals

2. Identifying critical user journeys

3. Having user empathy. Being able to think like someone who has *never* seen the product before.

4. Understanding psychology and the ways product design can influence human perception

Your end goal should be that you could see any product, and immediately critique its structure, layout, visuals, interaction patterns, and more. This will be invaluable in interviews and in your day to day life as a product manager.

Analytical Thinking

Analytical thinking is all about taking a vaguely defined problem, distilling it into all of its subcomponents, analyzing each one, and then aggregating those analyses into an overall conclusion. In other words, can you take a complicated problem and methodically approach it in a way that allows you to reach an effective solution?

As a product manager, you will constantly face exceedingly complicated problems. For instance, let's say you work on a music streaming service, and your product is doing great in most places, but in India, a competitor has most of the market share.

Why is that? Can you come up with a series of analyses you would perform and questions you might ask to answer that?

One hypothesis might be that this is due to cultural differences in this market. It's possible that user preferences about design are different there. How would you determine that?

Or, maybe there are distinct user needs in India. For instance, maybe features focused on offline listening are much more important due to more expensive cellular data and worse connectivity, and your product doesn't focus on this enough. How would you research this hypothesis?

It could be a strategic issue. Maybe the competitor has certain partnerships in India that drive a lot of usage of their product. What data could you look at to validate this hypothesis?

It could also be a discoverability issue. Maybe your product marketing and growth strategy doesn't work well in that market. What steps would you take to confirm or deny this idea?

This type of thinking is central to being a product manager. One of your core responsibilities is to identify major opportunities or issues with your product and figure out a broad strategy and vision to address them. The only way to efficiently tackle these vague problems is to be an analytical thinker. You need to be someone who can identify all the components of a given problem and figure out how to analyze them.

So, how do you develop this skill in college? **Put yourself in situations where you are responsible for solving a large, complex problem on your own.** In general, the best way to do this is to find leadership roles within some club, extracurricular activity, internship, or side project.

As a rule of thumb, if your first response to some task or problem is "How on earth do I solve that?", then it is likely a good opportunity to develop your analytical thinking. Don't be afraid of situations where you feel uncomfortable, or in a little bit over your head, or unsure of what to do. As a Product Manager, you will constantly face situations and problems like this (it is literally your job).

You can also develop analytical thinking by analyzing how other people break down complicated problems. Read essays, blogs, or articles that attempt to tackle a really open problem space. As you read, pay close attention to how they frame the problem and analyze it. What do they consider? What data do they look at? How do they aggregate the data to come to a broader conclusion?

As an example, content written by venture capitalists often demonstrates analytical thinking very well. Venture capitalists' job is to dive deep into brand new areas of technology, using an analytical framework in order to identify which companies tackling that problem space are worth investing in. Reading some VC investment memos or pitches is therefore a great way to improve your own analytical thinking skills.

Try to set some goals in this area by the end of college, such as:

1. Get to the point where a friend could ask you a broad, case style question about some company, and you could provide a compelling, off-the-cuff answer without breaking a sweat

2. Have 3-5 stories of instances where you were in charge of solving a big problem. Be able to talk through *exactly* how you approached it and solved it.

These skills and stories will be invaluable for both your interviews and your eventual job as a product manager.

Technical Skills

Finally, there are some expectations of technical skills for most entry level product manager jobs. Because a significant portion of your time will be spent working with software engineers, it's crucial you can understand their language.

If you have no idea how software is built, you will have a very hard time being an effective product manager. You won't be able to make the right product decisions based on engineering tradeoffs. You won't be able to influence your engineering team because they will not trust or respect you. Finally, you won't be able to fully grasp the non user-facing development work that may be critical to your product.

In particular, we recommend you focus on developing the following technical skills in college:

1. **Data structures and algorithms** - have a very strong understanding of all of the core data structures and how to manipulate them. Be able to solve problems algorithmically.

2. **System design** - be able to take a broad problem statement, and talk through all of the components that would need to work together in order to build that system. In addition, develop a strong understanding of core system design concepts, such as client vs. server, caching

3. **Databases** - have some knowledge of how data is stored, queried, and analyzed.

There are a number of ways to learn these skills. The easiest way is to take all of the core computer science classes in college (a later section of this book will touch more deeply on classes to consider taking in college).

However, that is not the only way. Another good approach is to do some side projects. **We highly recommend writing a full stack application that involves client code, server code, and a database.** It doesn't need to be super complicated or some amazing product. The goal is simply to have built an application from end-to-end. You will learn so much from doing this. It basically ensures that you fundamentally understand how most software applications work.

There are also several online courses and websites that help develop computer science fundamentals, from algorithmic heavy websites like Leetcode to more traditional course-style work such as Coursera and Udemy. These resources can also be helpful.

Remember that as a product manager, you do not have to be the *expert* at any of these technical topics. You simply need to:

1. Understand the implications a product decision has on engineering resources

2. Understand how a given system design will influence the user-facing aspects of a product

3. Understand what the engineers you work with are saying

Figure out the right set of activities (whether that be classes, courses, books, side projects, or something else) that allow you to achieve these goals.

—

At this point, we hope that you have a crystal clear understanding of the skills you will need to demonstrate on your resume, in interviews, and on the job. Now, you just need to figure out the activities you could pursue that will let you develop and highlight these skills.

The rest of this chapter will focus on helping you do just that. We will give you examples of classes, extracurriculars, and internships that could fit very well into someone's path to becoming a product manager straight out of college.

However, please remember that these are just examples. They are meant to be illustrative, not prescriptive. There is no single path to becoming a product manager, so try to develop these skills in a way that uniquely fits your interests and story.

Chapter 8

Classes to Take

There is no specific course that will make or break your product management career. However, there are certainly *types* of courses that we've found to be useful in our jobs.

In this section, we'll break down a few different types of courses that may help you in your path to breaking into product management.

Please note that we are not recommending you to do *all* of these (in fact, taking all of these will likely be impossible). Rather, use this list as a sounding board for classes you may want to take if they pique your interest, and as a way to learn how certain types of classes will apply to product management.

Computer Science

When companies say they are looking for product managers that are technical, they are mostly concerned with the ability for a product manager to communicate effectively with engineers.

Taking computer science courses will help you be effective as a product manager in two ways:

1. It will give you the computer science foundation necessary to understand high-level technical concepts and constraints. Having the same technical vocabulary as engineers is important.

2. It will allow you to get your hands dirty and do some engineering work so that when become a product manager, you will better understand engineering tradeoffs and the challenges that engineers may face. You will have *empathy* for your engineering team.

When deciding which computer science courses to take, try to get a combination of theory and application. You want to take the foundational theory classes, but you also want to have some direct experience doing software development.

In general, we *highly* recommend you take the "core" computer science curriculum which looks something like the following at most schools:

1. Intro to Computer Science

2. Data Structures and Algorithms

3. Operating Systems

4. Software Design

5. Databases

6. Advanced Algorithms

If you take a core set of classes like the above, you will almost certainly have the technical background you need to be an effective product manager. These classes are the closest you will get to "required" classes for becoming a product manager out of college (but even then, it is possible to become one without them).

If you have the opportunity to take a few additional computer science classes, we recommend looking for classes with the following traits:

1. Classes that involves working on a team (e.g. large, group based software design)

2. Classes that involve building a product from end-to-end (e.g. a capstone project where you build a full stack application and think about both the product design as well as the technical implementation)

3. Classes that help develop familiarity with specific computer science skill sets (such as machine learning)

Note that you do not need to be a computer science major to become a PM out of college. Given that the core computer science curriculum is really just 5 or so key classes, you can easily develop a strong technical background with just a minor. This is especially true if you are also developing CS skills via other methods, such as side projects.

Many companies recruiting APMs out of college do not have specific technical requirements (the *notable* exception being Google, which has historically required at least a minor). What matters is that on your resume, and in your interviews, you can demonstrate you have enough of a technical background.

That said, doing at least a minor will likely make your life easier. It is a much simpler way of conveying on your resume that you have technical chops than trying to convince the recruiter your side project was sufficiently complex.

Math and Statistics

Most good product managers are very data driven. They can manipulate numbers well, and understand how to think through what data means (and doesn't mean). A strong background in statistics or math can help develop these skills a lot.

We would recommend sticking with the basics here - real analysis isn't really going to help you much. But, the basics of calculus, linear algebra, probability, experimental design, and data science may be useful.

Math classes will help you develop regimented thinking about numbers and logic, whereas statistics classes will help you understand how to think about collecting data and analyzing it.

You will run a lot of experiments as a product manager, so experimental design in particular is a very transferable skill. Knowing when is a result statistically significant vs. not, how to ensure an experimental is probably set-up to create valid results, and how to express data in terms of confidence intervals is exceedingly valuable.

A class that teaches you some basic data analysis toolkits can also be useful. Tools like R, Python, Stata, and Tableau are used very widely for data analysis, and many product managers do this type data analysis themselves.

Economics

Having a foundation in basic economic theory can be helpful. For instance, concepts like opportunity cost and expected value come up frequently for product managers when they are prioritizing between features.

Similarly, a lot of economics is focused around incentives and how different incentive structures in marketplaces lead to certain outcomes. This type of regimented thinking is extremely useful if you ever end up working on a product that involves a complex ecosystem of participants.

For instance, if you work on Android, almost every decision you make involves thinking through the impact on:

1. Carriers like Verizon or Sprint

2. Device manufacturers like Samsung or Huawei

3. Competitor operating systems like Apple's iOS

4. Developers

5. End users

Taking a few basic classes on micro and macroeconomics will likely improve your ability to think strategically about ecosystems like that.

Psychology

A lot of product design revolves around consumer psychology. Understanding humans' irrationality and cognitive biases will likely improve your ability to create products.

A funny product story that illustrates this point is that of the loading spinner. A lot of airline ticket websites used to show the results almost immediately after the user initiated a search, showing only the minimal loading necessary. This makes intuitive sense - you want to show users results as fast as you can, right?

However, it turns out that these websites see higher engagement if they purposefully show the loading spinner for longer than is technically needed. Why? The hypothesis is that a longer loading time makes users feel like the website is doing something complicated behind the scenes. It feels like the website is really searching hard for the best deals.

There are tons of stories in the design world like this - cases where a product was better off showing an unnecessary loading state, or taking a bit longer than it really needs it.

The broader point is that you can't just make product decisions based on the assumption that humans are rational. A really common mistake in product design is having too much of a "logical" engineering mindset.

If you take a few introductory courses on human behavior, decision making, or cognitive biases, you will be introduced to a wealth of stories like these. Hopefully, they'll make you think twice the next time you are designing a new feature, and consider all the different ways people might react in an unexpected way.

Strategy, Sales, and Marketing

If you attend a university with an undergraduate business school, try to take advantage of some courses in the areas of strategy, sales, marketing, and other traditional business disciplines.

As a product manager, a lot of your work will revolve around setting your team's overall roadmap. To do this well, you need to be an effective strategic thinker. Having a good baseline understanding of business strategy and competitive forces will enable you to not only better communicate with senior leadership (which you will need to do a lot as a product manager), but will also allow you to craft a better product vision.

One issue some product managers face, particularly PMs who were formerly engineers, is that they are very good at the details of executing and building specific features, but they don't have the right strategic mindset. They can't appropriately identify the broader trends in their feature area or industry and make sure the team is going in the right high level direction.

A few strategy classes alone are not going to make you an excellent strategic thinker, but they certainly won't hurt. At minimum, you'll get exposure to the ways people analyze complex business dynamics, and you'll likely be able to apply that in some way to your job in the future.

Marketing and sales classes can also be useful because your job as a product manager will often involve interacting with these functional areas.

Product and marketing work together very closely to make sure what is being built matches what people want, and to ensure that marketing can appropriately frame and pitch the features being built. Familiarity with a marketing mindset will improve your ability to collaborate with a marketing team.

Similarly, understanding sales will help you a lot if you work in a sales-driven product organization such as cloud infrastructure or enterprise software-as-a-service. You may need to be part of sales pitches or client visits, acting as a product expert to help convince the client to purchase. Or, you may regularly sync with the sales team to better understand what features they think would drive more sales, and figure out how they fit into the product roadmap.

Public Speaking

Most people are scared to death of public speaking. However, as a product manager, you have to do it *a lot*. You will run virtually every meeting you are part of, and you will lead your team's reviews with senior executives.

Most colleges have some form of public speaking class. Taking it will help a lot with developing presentation and communication skills, as well as with getting over any fears you have of public speaking.

If your school doesn't have a public speaking class, then a good alternative is any class that involves a lot of presentations. It doesn't really matter what the topic is. Just find ways to put yourself in front of a group of people, and try to persuade or convince them of something. Believe us, you will be glad you did once you become a product manager.

Design

Being good at product design is absolutely integral to being an effective product manager. In almost any PM role, not only will designers be some of your closest collaborators, but you will often have to do a lot of design work yourself.

You might be doing basic mocks or sketches to pitch a high level product idea. Or, you may be testing your product, and you'll need to think with a design mindset about which flows work well versus which flows are confusing or cumbersome.

Any class that helps develop a design mindset will help you a lot with this. Study why things are built in a certain way, and all the decisions and logic that go into that. It doesn't need to be a tech product - all that matters is that you dig deep into how different design decisions impact the way a product is used and perceived by its users.

As a slightly trivial example, a class that spends 5 months teaching you about the history of chair design would likely be extremely useful. You probably think through:

1. The purpose of a chair

2. The use cases of a chair (e.g. home, restaurant, beach, etc)

3. The different design decisions involved in creating a chair, and the tradeoffs inherent in them, such as:

   a. How many legs?

   b. What is the shape of the seat?

   c. Should it have a back?

    d.   What materials can we use?

    e.   How expensive should it be?

    f.   How big should it be?

    g.   etc

4. The types of users that you can target with different kinds of chairs

5. How people use chairs

    a.   Do they *just* sit in them, or do they also lay in them?

    b.   How does a person typically sit in a chair? Does it differ for different ages, genders, cultures, locations, etc?

We could keep going! The point is that there is a lot of value in learning how to think in a structured and regimented way about product design (sometimes called "design thinking"), and that any class which digs deep on the design of something will help you develop this skill.

You want to internalize the core principles of design, such as: thinking about different types of users and use cases, identifying all the surprising ways people might use your product, being clear about design goals and non-goals, and articulating the tradeoffs between different design decisions.

These skills will be immensely useful in any product management job.

Other Courses

Good product managers have diverse and unique perspectives. Making good products is all about understanding users, and the problem that most of us face is that it's hard to think like people who are not like us.

The wider the range of experiences, ideas, and thought processes you have seen, the better you will be at empathizing with the largest possible range of users.

Take classes that interest you that aren't on our list.

In his famous Stanford commencement speech, Steve Jobs once shared that the class which had the biggest impact on his work at Apple was his calligraphy class. [3] It gave him a unique perspective that influenced the products he built in a way that other people and companies could not replicate.

We hope that you follow his advice. Although there are clear product management skills you can develop with classes in college, you should also have a goal of broadening your perspective as much as possible.

---

[3] Steve Jobs' Stanford Commencement Speech, 2005

Chapter 9

Extracurriculars

While classes can be useful in becoming a product manager, in many respects extracurriculars are more important.

Because so many of the core skills involved in being a product manager are either not taught in classrooms or are hard to develop in classrooms (e.g. leadership), extracurriculars are an excellent opportunity to make yourself stand out. They will help greatly with both your personal development, and with crafting a resume that gets you interviews.

In general, there are three primary categories of activities you may want to pursue outside of classes, each of which is more suited to learning certain types of skills (note that this list does not include internships, which we will cover in detail later this chapter):

1. Clubs

2. Personal projects

3. Self-directed learning

We'll go through some key examples of good opportunities in each category for developing product management skills.

Clubs

Most universities have a large number of extracurricular clubs and student groups, ranging from finance, to robotics, to community service, and everything in between.

While specific types of clubs can be useful in becoming a product manager, we have a higher order recommendation: **find any club or group you are interested in, and become a leader in it**.

At the end of the day, developing and demonstrating leadership, management, and similar skills is far more important than saying you were in a particular club. Plus, you are going to be more likely to have fun and do well if you pursue something that you feel passionate about.

Do you love the ecology and the environment? We bet your college has a bunch of other students who are also interested. Find whatever club exists (or create a new one), figure out ways you all can make an impact in the community and on campus, organize the members, and execute on your plan.

It won't matter that ecology, for the most part, has nothing to do with product management. Going through the above process will not only give you a fantastic story for interviews, but will help you get better at organization, leadership, and execution among a large group of people.

That being said, here are a few specific types of clubs that are particularly common and which we think are good starting options for most people interested in product management:

1. **Robotics or Engineering Clubs** - A lot of schools have student organizations oriented around building interesting robots or technical systems, and then competing with them. These are particularly transferable to being a PM since engineering is so core to what you work on.

2. **Business or Consulting Clubs** - Look out for groups that do consulting style work for local businesses. This is a great way to tackle "real world" business problems that you won't typically find in a more traditional academic setting.

3. **Entrepreneurship Clubs** - Most schools have groups of people who work together to come up with small business ideas, and try to build them out. This is a great way to develop a wide range of skills such as product design, marketing, sales, operations, and more.

4. **Student Government** - While student government is sometimes made fun of, in some schools the more senior positions entail a *lot* of leadership and responsibility. You'll interact with senior administrators, you'll drive efforts on campus, and you'll have to lead committees or teams.

5. **Major Campus Organizations** - Look out for the key 3-5 student groups at your school. Every school has a few major organizations which manage most of what happens on campus. These are often tied to any "student fees" paid as part of your tuition. For example, a club that takes some portion of the student fees and hosts all of the big events on campus each year (such as concerts, etc) is a good option. Clubs like this are

typically good opportunities because they have established leadership opportunities, they involve a lot of interaction with senior school administrators, and there is extremely low risk of the group falling apart.

These are just a few examples. The high level framework we recommend is to read through the "Key skills to develop in college" section of this book, and find the intersection of those skills with the things you are passionate about and which are available at your school.

Personal Projects

Personal projects are a great way to both explore areas you are interested in, as well as develop some of the specific skills that are useful as a product manager. Their downside relative to clubs and other group activities is that you likely won't develop as many interpersonal skills. However, the upside is that you have almost complete freedom in terms of what you work on, rather than being limited by what's available or popular at your school.

Similar to clubs, the projects you choose to pursue don't really need to focus on a particular topic. Rather, you want to simply ensure that you are developing PM skills within the context of the areas you find interesting.

With that said, here are a few types of projects which we think typically make sense for aspiring product managers:

1. **Coding Projects** - Build a simple app or a website. If possible, focus more on creating an end-to-end product than on showing off a particular type of technology.

2. **Data Analysis Projects** - There are thousands of interesting data sets available out there. Take one and dig into it with the tool of your choice (e.g. Excel, Python, Stata, R, SQL, Tableau). Try to come up with interesting *insights* from the data, rather than just share basic metrics from the data. Compile your results into a blog post or a presentation that you can link to and share with others.

3. **Design Projects** - Learn a design tool such as Sketch, and then do design work for classmates or for clubs at your school. Or, even better, do freelance design work for local small businesses. Host your portfolio online, and for each set of designs do a quick write-up on the design thinking that led to that result, and the impact the design had.

4. **Strategy Projects** - If you enjoy thinking about industries or companies strategically, turn that passion into an online blog where you write out theses about companies or industries. As an example - check out the investment thesis decks that a lot of venture capitalists produce online. Or, create Youtube videos where you breakdown and analyze companies or products (as an example, check out Scott Galloways' L2 Inc Youtube channel[4]).

---

[4] L2inc Youtube Channel by Scott Galloway

5. **Start a small business** - Don't be intimidated by this; you don't need to found a startup that raises VC funding. *Anyone* can start a very basic business online. Like making things? Start a shop on Etsy. Interesting in E-commerce? Dropship on Amazon. Enjoy writing? Write an e-book or be a guest contributor to online magazines. Or, set-up a small business in your school, providing a basic service for classmates. What matters is that you create something and go through the process of marketing and selling it.

For all of these personal projects, try to have an artifact that you can share with someone (like a recruiter) which demonstrates what you did. This might be a link to a blog, a YouTube channel, a book, a design portfolio, a slide-deck that summarizes an analysis, or a publication in a magazine. For a coding project, don't just link to Github - either let the user try the product out themselves on a website, or at least have a video which shows the product working. Remember that you're trying to show off *product* skills, not just technical ones.

Hopefully, you find these side projects to be fun! You can apply the categories of projects we listed to almost any vertical area - the environment, politics, blockchain, real estate, etc. So, craft your side projects in a way that both demonstrates the key PM skills as well as touches on the topics you care about. If you do this, your side projects will help you stand out much more as an applicant, because they provide a great medium to show off your unique interests and story.

Self-Directed Learning

While school can teach you many things, there is a lot of knowledge which is not readily taught in the classroom, but which is immensely useful as you go through the product management recruiting process and eventually work as a product manager.

First and foremost, an aspiring product manager you should have a good baseline understanding of what is happening in the tech industry. This includes topics such as the technologies (e.g. machine learning, augmented and virtual reality), the companies (which are the "hot" startups? Who are the major incumbents? Who is IPOing?), the investors (where is the money going? What are the investment theses? Which companies are raising capital?), and the leaders (what is the top talent saying and doing?).

While your knowledge of many of these topics can be high level, it is critical that you have at least a solid overview of the space. The best way to develop this overview is to follow the key technology newsletters, publications, podcasts, and blogs.

We highly recommend the following as good starting points:

1. **Stratechery** - Excellent commentary on business strategy in the tech industry by Ben Thompson.

2. **Axios Pro Rata and Login** - Daily summary of venture capital deals and funding in the tech world, and tech news, respectively.

3. **Fortune Data Sheet and Term Sheet** - Fortune's daily newsletter covering the business of tech and VC/PE funding, respectively.

4. **CB Insights** - Extremely analytical deep dives into segments of the tech industry, e.g. "Blockchain in healthcare report"

5. **Pitchbook News** - Good source of tech and business news, written from an investor's angle.

6. **Strictly VC** - Daily summary of happenings in the venture capital world.

7. **Andrew Chen's Newsletter** - Andrew is a partner at Andreessen Horowitz and writes essays mostly focused on macro analysis of trends in the tech industry.

8. **The a16z (Andreessen Horowitz) Podcast and Newsletter** - they put out a ton of great content covering basically every angle of technology.

9. If you're particularly interested in the perspective of venture capitalists, you may want to subscribe to **Brad Feld's newsletter, Tomasz Tunguz' newsletter**, or **Fred Wilson's newsletter**

Second, you should follow the specific verticals which you are particularly interested in more deeply. Have one to two areas where you could be considered more of a "domain expert" rather than just a generalist. Get deep in these areas - you should know exactly what is going on, what major problems are being solved, the subtle nuances of each company's strategy, and the who the key thought leaders are.

Books and online courses are often a great starting point for developing this type of knowledge. Check out the top books on Amazon as well as the top classes in places like Coursera, Udemy, EdX, and the litany of other platforms for online learning. For instance, if you're interested in machine learning, you should probably take Andrew Ng's introduction to machine learning class on Coursera.

However, to truly be a domain expert you need to push beyond this. Books and classes will always lag behind the bleeding edge of an industry. So, find the leading people in the fields you're interested in, and follow them on the platforms where they put out content regularly. Look out for personal blogs, Medium accounts, twitter posts, podcasts, or newsletters by those leaders. This will give you, by far, the most up-to-date insights on what they're thinking, and where that area is going.

For example, if you're interested in the blockchain space, you better be following content like Anthony Pompliano's podcast and newsletter, the Multicoin Capital blog, the "51percent" podcast, Delphi Digital's publications, Chris Dixon's content, and a whole lot more.

It can also be useful to look for in person events (such as conferences) in your target niches. These can be great opportunities to meet and learn from experts who might not otherwise publicly post their thoughts or opinions.

The third type of knowledge which is worth pursuing outside of the classroom is knowledge about specific products. As a product manager, it's very helpful to have a good understanding of what all the leading companies are doing in terms of product design and product strategy. This will help you in both interviews and in a job, because it gives you references to learn from and be inspired by.

For example, let's say you end up working at a company with some sort of personalized feed in its product. If you are very familiar with Facebook, Quora, Google News, and other existing "feed" products, you'll be very well positioned to do well. You'll know the best practices and you'll have seen different approaches that companies take, allowing you to reach much more informed, intelligent decisions for your own product.

Similarly, during an interview, it looks great when you are talking through a question and can reference how other companies have handled similar situations. From there, you can talk through the pros and cons of each approach, and determine what makes the most sense for the question at hand.

The best way to gain this type of knowledge is by being an early adopter of tech products. If you read about an app or a new company, spend 20 minutes trying it out and thinking about what makes it unique. What niche are they targeting? What trends are they trying to ride? Do they do anything novel in terms of product design?

Similarly, if you see a product that you use a lot launch a new feature, spend your commute the next day talking to yourself about why they would have specifically chosen to launch that feature in that way.

The final type of knowledge which can be hard to gain directly from classes are "tools" which may be useful on the job. For example, Sketch, Photoshop, and other design tools are often used by product managers for creating wireframes. Data tools like R, Python, Tableau, and SQL are often used by product managers to run data analyses.

These toolsets all have tons of tutorials on the internet - just lookup courses or tutorials for the tools of your choice.

We would recommend, at minimum, that you become familiar with at least 1 wireframing tool (Sketch is our #1 recommendation, InVision is also good), and at least one data analysis tool/language (SQL is our #1 recommendation, Tableau is also great). Although being familiar with these tools is certainly not required for many product manager jobs, it will help you stand out, and it will also make your life a lot easier once you start working.

Chapter 10

Internships

So far in this chapter, we've given you a rundown of key skills to develop, classes to take, and extracurricular projects to pursue. However, at the end of the day, the biggest contributor to getting a PM job out of college is having good internships.

Internships are not only one of the best ways to signal that you have the right background for a job in product management, but they are also a great way to gather valuable experiences working with others professionally. These experiences will not only help you develop several key product manager skills, but they can also form the basis of great stories for behavioral interviews.

The question we get most often regarding internships is: what is the optimal internship for someone who wants to be a product manager? The seemingly obvious answer is a product management internship, but the truth is more nuanced than that.

While a product management internship is certainly a great way to prepare yourself for a product management job out of college, there are a lot of other compelling options as well. In this section we'll explore what to look for in an internship, the best types of internships for aspiring product managers, and how to make the most of whatever internships you end up with.

Key Characteristics to Look for in an Internship

As we've discussed many times, the #1 thing you should consider when making any decision about becoming a product manager is the skill-set you need to develop and demonstrate. There are hundreds of internships which you could reasonably argue will help you in being a product manager. We can't list all of them, so instead our best piece of advice is to focus on finding internships which will develop the key skills we mentioned earlier in this book:

1. Leadership

2. Communication

3. Product Strategy and Design

4. Analytical Thinking

5. Technical Skills

So, how do these skills surface in internships? What sorts of characteristics might indicate an internship is a good fit for becoming a product manager?

For leadership, try to find a job that revolves around interfacing with or influencing an array of people. Ideally, you work on a project that requires support or buy-in from multiple stakeholders. Or, you lead an initiative that many people have to contribute to.

For communication, your job responsibilities should include presenting, pitching, or facilitating conversation. This could be realized in a number of ways. Maybe you are working with clients and need to sell them something. Maybe you have to run a ton of meetings or create alignment between different teams with different interests. Or, maybe you have to present your research or ideas to senior people at the company a few times over the summer.

For product strategy and design, ideally you have a job where you either work on high level strategic planning for a company, or where you get down into the details of influencing the way a product works or looks. This does not necessarily need to involve a tech product - it simply needs to help you develop either strategic or design thinking.

For analytical thinking, you want to look for an internship where you will be in charge of analyzing a complex situation, involving many data points or players, where you have to synthesize everything into a conclusion.

Finally, for technical skills, you want to look for a job that involves working with computer science or software engineers in some way.

If you're asking yourself "What job has *all* of those things?", don't fret. Your internships don't need to develop or demonstrate *all* of these skills. Instead, just try to make sure that whatever jobs you do during college cover at least a couple of these skills. Then, use your extracurriculars, classes, and personal projects to cover what your internships missed.

Plus, as a college student, you have three internship opportunities. So, it's totally alright if each one has a different area of focus. By the time you are a senior applying to new grad product manager programs, you will have hopefully developed and demonstrated most of these skills.

Keep in mind that developing these skills during your internship is not just a matter of applying to the right roles. You need to be *deliberate* during your internships about making sure you develop the right set of skills. Talk to your manager early and tell him or her what you want to gain from the internship.

For instance, almost any internship could involve presenting to some senior people at your company, discussing what you achieved during the summer. This is a great way to work on your presentation and communication skills. So, at the beginning of your internship, tell your manager you want to do this!

Similarly, in addition to your primary project, you could work on the side during your internship to identify a problem with your company, and do some analysis (competitive research, data analysis, user studies, etc) to come up with a possible solution. Then, share a deck of your findings with your co-workers to see if they agree. If you did a good job, they'll like it, and you can say you proactively identified an issue and found a solution - clearly demonstrating analytical thinking and entrepreneurial ability.

This mentality will allow you to craft your internships into the best possible experiences they can be in terms of preparing you to become a product manager.

Finally, you should also use this list of characteristics as a guide for how you talk about your internships on your resume or during interviews. Frame your experiences in terms of these skills.

With all of that said, you now hopefully understand how to think about internships from the perspective of the skills to look for and develop. We'll now quickly highlight some of the most common internships paths for aspiring product managers.

Product Management Internships

The most obvious way to become a full time product manager is to be a product management intern. You'll see what the job is like, you'll develop the right skills, and you will have a high chance of getting a return offer assuming you do well.

However, you do not *need* a product management internship to become a PM out of college. In fact, there are three keys reasons why it may not make sense for you to pursue a product management internship.

First, there simply aren't that many PM internship programs for undergraduate students. If you think being a product manager out of college is competitive, try becoming a PM intern.

The reason for this is that it is very, very hard to craft a PM internship that sets someone up for success. So much of being a PM revolves around context, relationships, and trust, and it honestly probably takes at least 3 months at a given company before you have developed those, *especially* as someone fresh out of college.

As a result, even among the companies that offer new grad product manager programs, very few offer internships. For example, Facebook used to have a rotational product manager internship, but does not anymore, because it wasn't productive for either the interns or for Facebook.

Furthermore, if a company does offer a PM internship, it will almost certainly only be available to students in their third summer (aka their junior summer), and not to anyone younger. As such, you will need to find other types of internships when you are earlier in your college career.

Note that given the lack of product management internships available, **no company will expect you to have had a PM internship during college when you apply to their full time PM program**.

The second reason it doesn't always make sense to pursue a product management internship is that PM internships are not very representative of what the full time role is like. Because it takes so long to develop the basic context and trust needed to become an effective PM, PM internships can often feel very different from what it is like to be a full time product manager.

Compare this dynamic to a software engineering internship, where you can almost guarantee you will see exactly what it is like to be a full time software engineer. The software engineering job requires much less "ramp up" time.

As such, one could make the argument that you are better off doing an internship where less time is "wasted", and where you can more directly gather data points about what a specific type of job will be like after college. After all, a key purpose of internships is figuring out what you want to do in your career.

The third reason it may not make sense to pursue a PM internship is that having non-PM experiences can be very valuable once you become a full time product manager. For instance, many people would say you are better off interning as a software engineer before becoming a product manager, since you will work so much with software engineers.

Similarly, interning as a product designer will likely give you a unique skill-set which sets you apart as a product manager.

Our point is not that you should avoid a PM internship. If you can get one and you want to do it, do it! But, if you can't get one, or if you want to try out another job to see if you like it, that is also totally fine. **You do not *need* to have been a PM intern to break into product management out of college.** In fact, we would guess that more new grad product managers have non-PM internship backgrounds than have PM internship backgrounds.

Focus on developing PM skills and exploring different possible passions during your internships. It's fine to wait to focus on landing a product management job until you are in your senior year.

Software Engineering Internships

Probably the most common internship for aspiring product managers is software engineering. While the job of a software engineer differs wildly from that of a product manager, there are tons of advantages to interning as a software engineer if you eventually see yourself becoming a product manager. In fact, both of us were software engineering interns before we switched into product management.

New grad product management programs love to hire former software engineering interns because such internships are hard proof of your technical ability and your capacity to work with engineers. As we've discussed, one of your main responsibilities as a product manager is to work with software engineers, so being able to speak their language and understand technical tradeoffs is critical.

Another key benefit of a software engineering internship is that you're very close to the product. As a result, if you're diligent, you can identify opportunities to make or influence product decisions. This is a fantastic way to force yourself to think like a product manager. Don't just consider *how* to build your summer internship project, but also consider *what* should be built. Most teams will be really appreciative if you adopt this "product engineer" mindset and suggest areas where the product could be improved.

Finally, as a software engineering intern, you are likely to work with a product manager in some capacity. This is a great opportunity to learn by watching. Observe how they interact with the team, how they lead meetings, and how they pitch product ideas and product strategy. If you work closely with them, you could very well learn a lot about product management!

Design Internships

Interning as a designer in a tech company is another very common path to becoming a product manager. It is, in many ways, the other side of the coin to a software engineering internship. While you won't develop as much of a technical background, you will develop a lot of skills around product design.

Designers are probably the group of people which product managers spend the second most time with after engineers. The skills you develop will help you work with designers as a PM. For instance, being adept at doing quick mockups, sketches, and prototype flows is a *really* valuable skill which every product manager should have.

Furthermore, just like for a software engineering internship, it is highly likely you will work with product managers in a design internship, so once again you will be able to learn by observing.

Data Science or Business Analyst Internships

In virtually all tech companies, core product development teams are comprised of product managers, software engineers, designers, and data scientists.

As such, any data science or analytics focused role will both give you an inside look at what it is like to work with a PM, as well as help you develop data analysis skills.

Being data-driven is crucial as a product manager. Having a strong background in this area will help you a lot, both in terms of mindset (thinking about problems in terms of metrics) and in terms of toolkits (understanding and being adept with tools like SQL, Excel, Tableau, etc).

As a product manager, you won't always have a data scientist at your beck and call to run queries or pull statistics. Being someone who can do these things yourself is really valuable. Plus, having data makes your life so much simpler as a PM, since it's a lot easier to convince people to do things if you have hard numbers!

Finally, just like for design and software engineering internships, you are likely to work with a PM as a data scientist. So, it's a good way to see what the job is like and learn from someone more experienced.

Other Internships

Any internship that fosters interpersonal skills, analytical thinking, or strategic thinking can help you prepare for a product manager job. Some other common internships we see among new grad product managers are:

1. Product marketing

2. Program or project management

3. Management Consulting

4. Investment Banking

Overall, if you don't get a product management internship and want to try something other than software engineering, look for opportunities at the intersection of business, technology, and design. The title doesn't matter as much as the skill-set that you gain.

Chapter 11

Some Final Tips

Before discussing applying to jobs and landing an offer, we'll touch on a few final pieces of advice to consider as you work your way through college.

Be an Entrepreneur

There are a lot of parallels between great product managers and great entrepreneurs. Many graduates who go into product management have the specific intention of starting their own company later; this was true in each of our cases. Consider the following take from Ben Horowitz in his legendary essay, "Good Product Manager/Bad Product Manager".

"Good product managers know the market, the product, the product line and the competition extremely well and operate from a strong basis of knowledge and confidence.

A good product manager is the CEO of the product.

A good product manager takes full responsibility and measures themselves in terms of the success of the product."

Now imagine the phrase product manager being replaced by the word entrepreneur.

"Good entrepreneurs know the market, the product, the product line and the competition extremely well and operate from a strong basis of knowledge and confidence.

A good entrepreneur is the CEO of the product.

A good entrepreneur takes full responsibility and measures themselves in terms of the success of the product."

You can see the overlap between a great entrepreneur and a great product manager. Both are ultimately the responsible for the full experience which is created, and both need to take initiative and do whatever is needed to launch a great a product.

One of the best ways to practice product management is to build something from the ground up, launch it, and iterate and improve on it over time. College is an amazing time to do this - there is no other period in your life where trying something like this is as risk free. No matter whether you fail or succeed, you'll learn so much about product design, metrics, marketing, sales, user research, and more.

Remember that being an entrepreneur doesn't necessarily mean building an app and getting millions of users. We've met APMs who started designer sock websites, initiatives for social change, and even small consulting agencies for local businesses.

Anything you can do in college that will force you to take ownership of a project, learn from mistakes, and empathize with your customers will go a long way towards helping you become a better product manager.

What GPA do I need?

On one hand, your GPA alone will not get you a job as a PM. In fact, for the most part your GPA will only help with getting an interview, and will have very little bearing on getting an offer. Furthermore, a GPA above a certain bar will only have marginal benefits (e.g. a 4.0 won't be perceived that differently from a 3.8).

On the other hand, a low GPA will definitely make your life harder. Because there are so few PM roles out of college, and because these roles are so competitive, you will be up against a vast pool of candidates with 3.7+ GPAs. Having a GPA of ~3.3 or lower will make it really tough for you to get an interview.

Our overall recommendation is to try to have GPA of at least 3.5 - 3.7 - you'll be glad you do once you start applying to jobs! That said, don't sacrifice side projects or extracurriculars just to get a 4.0, and don't avoid classes you think would be interesting or useful just because they may be hard and lower your GPA a little.

The final section of the book, Getting the Job, will cover more tips around how to apply to PM jobs if you do have a low GPA.

How technical do I need to be?

There is not a definitive answer to this question. The degree to which you need to be technical is highly dependent on the team that you're on. The more technical you are, the larger the number of PM roles you'll be able to perform in effectively.

For instance, some PM roles involve working on things such as developer tools, APIs, or machine learning based features. It would be exceptionally difficult to do this work without a technical background.

In contrast, someone working on the frontend of a consumer app like Snapchat does not need to be nearly as technical. That is not to say that a strong technical background would not help (no matter what you're always working with engineers), but it is less "required".

Ultimately, technical knowledge is just another tool in the product manager toolbox that can make you more effective in your role. With that said, as we mentioned earlier in the book, there is a baseline technical competency that most companies require in order to get a PM job out of college.

As a quick test, here are some basic questions you likely want to be able to answer as a PM:

- *What's the difference between a server and client?*

- *In what ways does creating a mobile application differ from creating a web app?*

- *What does it mean to cache something?*

- *What is a thread?*

- *Can you explain the basic data structures (array, list, hashmap, heap, stack, etc) and their purpose?*

- *Talk me through, end to end, what happens when I call an Uber.*

In addition, here are some nice-to-haves, which will certainly help in the job:

- Familiarity with SQL and the ability to write scripts

- An understanding of latency, memory consumption, and other performance-related topics

- Basic understanding of machine learning (What is a feature? A label? What does it mean to "train" a model? Could you explain gradient descent?)

If you are a computer science major and have done well in your classes and/or have done a software engineering internship - you are likely technical enough to be an new grad product manager. If you haven't done either of these things but you have a strong grasp of computer science fundamentals from programming on your own, you are also likely technical enough.

If you have done none of these things, then we have two pieces of advice:

1. Take some computer science classes or online courses, or do a computer science side project. Having *something* here is 10x better than having nothing at all.

2. Look for companies that don't explicitly require technical backgrounds in their new grad PM role. For instance, Google APM explicitly requires some sort of CS background, whereas

Facebook RPM is much more willing to hire non-technical people.

Finally, note that if you haven't formally studied computer science or done a software engineering internship, but you have some technical background, you should *make sure* that expertise comes out in your resume. Recruiters will filter out resumes if it doesn't look like the candidate has enough of a technical background. We'll cover this further in the Getting the Job section.

From the Insiders - 3rd Year Startup PM

"I'm almost never the most technical person in the room. What I do have, however, is the ability to understand engineering tradeoffs and problems well enough to make good product prioritization decisions. I understand enough to know what's easy, what's hard, and what's possible. This allows me to communicate effectively with my engineering team."

Part 3

Getting the Job

So far, you've learned what it's like to be a product manager, and you've learned how to prepare for a career in product management in college. However, your biggest challenge is going to be getting the job.

Product management jobs, especially for new graduates, are very competitive. Not only are the interviews challenging, but the mere process of getting an interview can be daunting to many potential applicants.

In this final chapter, we'll lay out everything you need to know about getting the job. We'll tell you exactly how to land an interview and get an offer, covering everything from how to structure your resume, to when to apply, to how to excel at product interviews.

Chapter 12

Before the Interview

Before you worry about doing well in PM interviews, you need to focus on getting an interview in the first place. Here are a few tips and tricks to keep in mind as you navigate the process.

When to Apply

In general, full time PM recruiting for college students tends to happen between July and September the year before you would start. So, if you are graduating in 2020, be ready to apply to companies by July 2019. (PM internship recruiting typically happens between September and December)

Note that many companies have very short windows where their new grad PM jobs are open for applications. For instance, historically, the Google APM role has only been available on Google's website for about 2 weeks in August. If you miss the deadline, you're out of luck.

Start checking the websites of companies you are interested in around July. Most will either list the dates their applications open, or will direct you to a social media page where they will announce when applications are open. Facebook, for instance, has a Facebook page for their RPM program where they announce it when you can apply.

It is also in your best interest to apply as early as possible. New grad PM positions are very competitive, and nearly all of these programs hire candidates on a rolling basis. We personally know multiple people who went through an entire interview process, and were then told that while the company would like to extend an offer, the class had already filled up, and so the company was unable to do so. Don't let this happen to you - plan to apply as soon as the applications open up.

Resume and Applications

Most applications for new grad PM jobs will only ask you for one thing: a resume. Your resume will be virtually the sole factor that determines whether you get an interview, so it is worth taking some time to make sure it is done well.

There is abundant information online and in books about how to write a good resume. In general, these resources recommend that you: use a simple and easy-to-read layout, outline *specific* accomplishments with precise explanations (e.g. Built X which achieved Y), only mention things that you could back up if asked about during an interview, and focus on real experiences rather than personal statements.

So, we won't go into detail about good *general* resume writing tips, but there are some specific things to keep in mind when crafting your resume for a PM job.

First and foremost, make sure you resume frames **everything** in terms of product management skills. Recruiters are primarily looking for evidence of the skills you will need to succeed at the job. As we've discussed, success as a PM is primarily as a result of: leadership, communication, product strategy and design, analytical thinking, and technical background. You should be able to point to every line on your resume and tell someone which skill it is highlighting, and how.

For leadership, focus on group projects you have been a part of and clubs or extracurriculars you have participated in. Try to emphasize concrete instances where you drove a project or initiative to completion, or where you took on some degree of responsibility for the group at large.

The subject matter of your leadership activity is not particularly important - it certainly does not need to be technology related. You could be a team captain for a sports team, have a senior position in the student government, or just be someone who helps manage or run various events. What matters is that you express to a recruiter who is reading your resume that you are capable of managing and leading others.

Leadership based bullet points on a resume will probably look something like:

Head of the robotics club. Managed weekly body meetings, fundraising, and our efforts to compete in Y robotics challenge. Team placed 3rd.

Managed partnerships for annual hackathon, securing ~30 sponsors each year totalling ~$50,000 in value.

Led a team of 8 students, coordinating all marketing and design for the student government.

For communication, try to highlight situations where you had to pitch or sell others, or where you had to coordinate or facilitate complicated discussions across a wide range of people. Bullets on a resume for communication might look something like:

Pitched business case in Accenture case competition. Won first place out of 10 teams.

Ran weekly student government meetings, owning weekly agenda and mediating often controversial discussions among 40+ students.

Pitched and sold over 50 clients for XYZ small business.

For product strategy and design, outline instances where you either helped solve strategic questions, or worked on the design or functionality of some product. Bullet points on a resume for this might look like:

Identified issue with XYZ as software engineering intern. Pitched potential solution to design team. Built and launched proposed feature.

Designed and built web-app which does XYZ (www.xyz.webapp.com).

Wrote 25+ blog posts (xyz.blog.com) analyzing the onboarding flow for common tech products.

For analytical ability, try to emphasize a major, classes, competitions, or even test scores that demonstrate you have a strong logical and mathematical mind. If you're an engineer or a CS major, this is probably as easy as just having a really good GPA.

However, if you have a non-traditional major, you will have to work a bit harder. Have you competed in any business strategy or case competitions? Did you win some award or do really well in one of your math, economics, or CS classes? Are you ranked in topcoder, hackerrank, or one of the other online coding competitions? Figure out how you can frame one of your achievements in terms of rigorous analytical thinking, and make sure to emphasize that. Because you don't have a traditional "analytical" major, you will need to go out of your way to prove that you have that skill-set.

Bullet points for analytical thinking might look like:

Major in Computer Science, 4.0/4.0 GPA

Wrote investment analysis for Self Driving Car industry, analyzing key players + important trends and proposing investments (link)

Wrote economics thesis on topic XYZ, involving statistical analysis of ABC data sets (link). Won award for best senior thesis in economics.

Finally, for technical ability, focus on classes or side projects where you either wrote code yourself, or worked very closely with other people writing code. Mention some personal coding projects, describe a time where you partnered with a software engineer to build something for a club, or list some complex things you had to do in your most difficult CS classes. Sample bullets for this might look like:

Used FIFA World Cup data to build a machine learning model which predicts how far a player will go based on their name (link)

Built web app which does XYZ (link).

Top 1000 on Leetcode - solved 100+ "Hard" problems

If you want to go above and beyond with your resume, consider creating a website showcasing the side projects that you've worked on as well as some of your interests and writing. Going through the additional effort of creating a portfolio can show your uniqueness as a candidate as well as your curiosity outside of the classroom.

As you review your resume before applying, read through each bullet, and ask yourself: "Would this help show a recruiter that I would be a good PM? Does this demonstrate leadership, analytical ability, technical prowess or one of the other critical PM skills?". Try to make sure the answer is a resounding **yes** for every single part of your resume.

In the next pages, we've included what our resumes looked like in college (note that they are not perfect - a good exercise would be to point out how they could be improved!). Use them to get a more concrete idea of how you might highlight your skills and experiences.

Davis Reed Treybig

davis.treybig@gmail.com

Education

Duke University, Durham, NC   Expected May 2016
- B.S.E. in Electrical and Computer Engineering and B.S. in Computer Science
- GPA: 4.0/4.0, GMAT: 780, SAT: 2380

Work Experience

Associate Product Manager Intern, *Google*   Summer 2015
- Took ownership of new internal data collection feature, including securing legal/privacy reviews, creating rollout roadmap, developing documentation and opt-in flow for testers, and managing tester relations
- Conducted competitive performance analysis of Chrome vs. Microsoft Edge, integrating results with existing Edge research to produce a high-level overview of key performance disparities between the browsers
- Researched feasibility of new Chrome feature to notify users of resource-hungry tabs, culminating in a final proposal suggesting not to pursue the feature given engineering and UI challenges

Software Engineering Intern, *TabbedOut*   Summer 2014
- Implemented the sharing and joining of restaurant tabs in app via Bluetooth Low Energy
- Completed a vendor evaluation of push notification services; collaborated with marketing team to integrate chosen provider into mobile app
- Designed a Bluetooth Beacon based notification system to alert users they are in a venue; built internal deployment tool for beacons

Sales and Product Marketing Intern, *Lithium Technologies*   Summer 2013
- Researched and compiled social media customer care statistics to assist sales team and improve website SEO
- Improved lead generation and lead nurturing through study of competitors' practices

Extracurricular

Chief Marketing Officer, Duke University Union   Fall 2015 – Spring 2016
- Led a team of 7 to coordinate marketing, design, and photography efforts for all 13 committees in Duke's largest student-run programming body

Chair, Student Organization Finance Committee   Fall 2014 – Spring 2015
- Directed a committee of 15 that ran all student group related processes at Duke, including managing $700,000 of funding annually
- Overhauled student group funding system by pitching and implementing new financing software

Technology Sphere Chair, *Duke Business Society Executive Board*   Spring 2014 – Spring 2016
- Planned and ran all technology-related events for Duke Business Society, focusing on career planning, skill development, and interview preparation for students interested in careers in technology.

Vice Chair of New Student Groups, Student Organization Finance Committee   Fall 2013 – Spring 2014
- Ran the training and application process for all new student groups at Duke
- Collaborated with Duke Student Government to draft and pass legislation for a student group de-chartering process, leading to the recovery of ~$40,000 annually

Awards and Competitions

Boston Consulting Group Case Competition, 1st place, Durham, NC   Spring 2014
Accenture Internship Case Competition, 1st place, Durham, NC   Spring 2014

Personal

Languages: Spanish (Conversational), Java (including Android), Objective C, Swift, MATLAB
Hobbies: Weightlifting, Reading (non-fiction books, magazines such as *Scientific American*, *Wired*, and *Discover*), Cooking (especially baking), Basketball

Alan Ni

Education
Duke University, *Bachelor of Science in Computer Science with a Minor in Economics*, Durham, NC *Expected May 201*
- **Cumulative GPA:** 3.9
- **Relevant Coursework:** Data Structures and Algorithms, Computational Microeconomics, Discrete Math for Computer Science, Computer Architecture, Web Development, Software Design and Implementation, Everything Data, Writing Software for Maintainability

Languages and Skills
- **Experienced:** Java, Python, Git, Django, Flask, Eclipse, Javascript
- **Intermediate:** Unix, HTML, CSS, Backbone, SQL, Bootstrap, Heroku, Stylus, Jade
- **Familiar:** iOS, Objective C, C, Dojo, jQuery, Axure, Wireframing, Scala

Software Portfolio
- **Website:** http://alanni.me
- **Github:** www.github.com/anni

Awards
- Kleiner Perkins Caufield & Byers Engineering Fellow
- Melissa and Doug Entrepreneur (one of twelve students at Duke selected for stipend and mentorship)
- PennApps Hackathon Finalist (one of 20 out of 200+ teams) and Best Use of Mashery API
- Award Winner at KPCB Fellows Pitch Competition, one out of four teams that received awards
- Best Intern Idea Pitch at Redfin

Work Experience
Coursera, *Software Engineering Intern*, Mountain View, CA — *June 2014-Presen*
- Created Course Stories feature that is shown to all learners who complete a course; collected over 2000 stories from learners in the first week's launch
- Took over In Class Quick Questions feature and increased the pilot from five courses to over forty
- Implemented and resolved over ten AB tests for frontend features

Redfin, *Software Engineering Intern*, Seattle, WA — *May 2013-August 201*
- Implemented real estate data importers for multi-million dollar expansion to San Antonio and Santa Barbara
- Designed and coded agent tool features that will be used by over 200 agents
- Decreased the load time of matchmaker agent tool by over five times by batching Ajax requests
- Worked in an agile development team and wrote production code that deployed every three weeks

Shoeboxed Inc., *Engineering and Customer Support Intern*, Durham, NC — *January 2013-April 201*
- Automated OS environment installation and documented installation steps for usage on 20+ workstations
- Took ownership of technical customer support in a startup environment

Micro-Consulting for North Carolina, *Technical Consulting Intern*, Durham, NC — *August 2012-April 20*
- Engaged biweekly with leaders of local non-profit, Preservation Durham, to discuss improving their technologies
- Developed customized Salesforce database and reports for Preservation Durham
- Applied Python regular expressions to scrub data for 3,000 contacts from the previous Preservation Durham database and imported contacts into new database

Duke University Computer Science, *Undergraduate Teaching Assistant*, Durham, NC — *August 2012-January 20*
- Led two 20-person lab recitations weekly and taught Python and introductory computer science concepts
- Tutored individuals for 4 hours weekly during office hours

Projects
- **SMSmart**, Flask, Python, Javascript, HTML, CSS. Gives feature phones smart phone capabilities like Yelp and Google Maps through a text message interface that uses the Twilio API to send and receive messages
- **Netfixxed**, Django, Python, CSS, SQLite, Bootstrap, jQuery, Javascript, HTML, Heroku. Aggregates Netflix movies from all different viewing regions into one place along with ratings and reviews

Referrals

Aside from having a good resume, the biggest factor in getting an interview at a company is whether or not you have a referral (and how good that referral is). **We cannot express how powerful referrals can be**. The worse your resume is, the more critical it is that you get a referral, as you might otherwise have no chance of getting an interview.

Virtually all major tech companies have an internal form that lets employees write a referral for a candidate who wants to apply. Employees are generally asked to write a little bit about the person they are referring, including how they know the candidate and why they think the candidate would be a good fit. Employees are also frequently given incentives if they refer someone who gets hired; many companies will offer between $2,000-$10,000 for a successful referral.

As such, note that employees generally want to refer you - they benefit a lot if you get hired! But, employees also don't want to refer candidates who they think might perform badly, because that can reflect poorly on them. As such, if you want a referral, you'll need to find someone who **knows you, has seen your work, and can speak highly of you**.

The best way to achieve this is to find someone at the company who you previously worked with in a class, a club, or some other extracurricular activity. The more that person can describe *specific examples* of things they have seen you do which impressed them, the better your referral will be, and the more likely the referral will amplify your application.

Your aim should be to find someone who can write a referral like this:

I worked with Davis in Y activity over a span of 9 months during my senior year. During this time, he particularly impressed me in terms of how he handled X. Doing X well was very complex as it involved managing Y different students and administrators, and getting them to all agree on a plan for Z. Davis did this faster, more efficiently, and more independently than any of the other students I saw in this role over the 3 years I was part of this club.

This is the type of referral that will actually lead to a higher chance of getting an interview. A recruiter can take this and make a case for why you would be a good fit for a PM role in spite of other, weaker areas of your application.

What will *not* work are referrals like the following:

I've been friends with Davis for a few years. He's a really nice, funny guy who would be a great fit at Google.

While it is perhaps better than nothing, a recruiter will have a hard time using that referral to influence an interview or hiring decision. It doesn't demonstrate that you have any of the core PM skills.

So, spend the time to find someone who can actually speak to your work, and get a good referral. If you do, you'll be far, far more likely to get an interview (assuming there are no other glaring holes in your background).

Which companies you should apply to?

There are a *lot* of companies out there that recruit entry level product managers today. As such, it's impossible for us to give you an exhaustive, up to date list. That being said, here are some of the most well-known companies that recruit new grad APMs as of 2019:

- *Google*

- *Facebook (Called "Rotational Product Manager" or "RPM")*

- *Uber*

- *LinkedIn*

- *Microsoft (called "Program Manager")*

- *Dropbox*

- *Workday (called "Rotational Product Manager")*

- *Square*

- *Redfin*

- *Dropbox*

- *Yelp*

- *Asana*

- *Headspace*

- *Fitbit*

- *Walmart (eCommerce division)*

- *Verizon*

- *Workday*

In general, you'll find their APM roles in the "Student"/"New Graduate", "Product", or "Engineering" sections of their career page. Remember that many of these roles are only listed from ~July to ~September, so check regularly during this time frame.

The smaller the company, the harder it will be for you to find a new grad product manager role. In very small companies, the CEO often plays the role of PM. In mid-size companies, there are often not resources to accommodate and train a less-experienced PM, particularly when exponential growth is happening and everyone needs to be able to handle their work fully independently.

As such, larger companies are more likely to have roles for new grad product managers. They have the resources to sustain official programs to mentor and train you (e.g. Google, Facebook). However, there are exceptions to every rule, so if you are dead set on becoming a PM at a smaller company, go for it. Just know that you will really need to hustle, and it will be an uphill battle to convince the company they should hire you as a new grad PM.

If you're interested in working in smaller companies, start by checking out their career pages and seeing what roles are available. If you don't see anything related to product management, email the company, express your interest and why you would be a good fit, and see what they say.

We highly recommend doing some serious research about the company beforehand in this case. You may want to consider putting together a few sample product proposals that you can share with them. Come up with a feature that you think they should build, and write up a pitch deck or a document that outlines the feature end-to-end. This will both demonstrate your commitment and interest, as well as highlight your product insight, and it will be invaluable in terms of convincing them to hire a young PM with minimal work experience.

Chapter 13

Conquering the PM Interview

At this point, you know the basics of the application process, such as how to craft a resume, how to get a referral, and the typical timelines. The next step is to prepare for the interview itself. Assuming you hear back from a company and they like your application, you will likely be asked to perform a couple of phone interviews, followed up by an "onsite" round of 3 to 5 in-person interviews.

These interviews can be quite challenging. Product management interviews are unique and very few people naturally excel at them. You have to prepare in order to do well.

In this section, we will highlight how to master the PM interview. We'll start by giving a broad overview of techniques you should use during product interviews. From there, we'll dig into specific examples of the types of questions you might see. Finally, once you have a good understanding of what the interviews are like themselves, we'll give you advice on how to prepare for them, including timelines and methods.

The basics of a PM interview

The first thing worth noting about product management interviews is that there is not a standard question. As a software engineer, there is a good chance you'll get asked about a sorting algorithm or a dynamic programming question, but as a product manager, there really isn't any guarantee you will get asked about any particular topic.

Interviewers can ask you everything from "Estimate how many gas stations are there in New York City" to "Who's Google's biggest competitor" to "How would you build the API for a payment service?" to "Tell me the top 5 topics the board of directors of Quora is discussing every meeting" to "Let's assume self-driving cars exist. Walk me through everything that would change in the Lyft product experience as a result".

So, what's the common thread? These companies are probing your ability to think like a product manager, which means they want to know whether you can reason through all the different facets of a product or business, starting from a high-level strategic perspective, and going all the way down into the details. They're evaluating whether you can analyze a broad array of multidisciplinary data points and ultimately come to a conclusion that you can sell the interviewer on.

While you have no guarantees on the specific topic you will be asked about (it could be Facebook's Newsfeed or it could be a children's library!), you do have a good idea of the *type* of analysis they will be asking you to do. You know you will you be asked broad questions about products and companies, and you know that you will need to provide an end-to-end analysis of that topic from strategic plans down to specific designs.

As a result, preparing for PM interviews is all about getting good at thinking and communicating like a product manager. Clear communication, structured analytical thinking, and product sense will be your most valuable assets. Use these skills to provide **structured, clearly articulated answers that break down every facet of a question, and then synthesize the analysis of each sub-component into a broader conclusion**.

As an example of what we mean, you will almost assuredly get asked a question roughly of the form "You're the PM or CEO of XYZ company. Talk me through the most important strategic initiatives for the product, and then walk me through the design of the first feature you would build in that area. Finally, tell me how you would launch it, and how you would measure success and failure". From there, you are likely to get minimal input or assistance from the interviewer - you have to drive the answer on your own.

A good response would start by analyzing the product/company at a high level, identifying different players in the ecosystem, the relevant tech trends, possible competitors, and more. From there, you would synthesize the different high-level strategic components into a strategic conclusion for the company - it should go forward with plan X for Y reasons.

Next, you would outline the possible features that make the most sense within that strategy. You would talk about key user needs and user journeys, highlight different creative ways to solve them, and compare the pros and cons of each, referencing design, engineering, marketing, sales, and other vertical areas which may be influenced by these features.

From this, you would come to a conclusion about the most important feature to prioritize, and start talking through how it would be built. What would it look like? What are different choices do you have and how would you make them (e.g. implementing the feature this way would be much more complicated for XYZ reasons technically, but would be a cleaner design)? What are the edge cases?

With a feature plan in place, you would talk through the metrics you would look at to determine success and failure, as well as how you would roll the feature out. You might highlight possible risks and how you would mitigate them, as well as the areas you would be highly attentive to feedback in, ready to change direction if needed.

Finally, you would summarize everything you have talked about so far, bringing it all together and talking about high-level next steps assuming the first feature goes well.

How do you put yourself in the position to give an analysis like this? While the rest of this chapter will talk through lots of specific tips and provide sample interview questions, the best way to prepare is to simply practice the above line of thinking regularly. Every time you try a new product, read about a new company, or use an app you love, spend 10-15 minutes answering the above question to yourself.

As you do this, pay attention to the following:

1. Is your answer structured into concrete pieces, or are you just saying whatever comes to mind?

2. Are you communicating clearly? Do you fumble your words, or is your speech elegant? Could someone who knows *nothing* about technology follow you?

3. Was your analysis comprehensive? Did you cover many different facets of the company or product in question, or did you spend too much time on just one piece?

4. Did you think *analytically*, synthesizing disparate pieces of analysis into broader conclusions?

If someone can ask you any broad question, and you can provide an answer with the above traits, you are in an excellent position to do well in PM interviews. You're also in a good position to work as a product manager. This type of thinking is something you will do every day; it is your job to think about your product strategically, define a vision or roadmap, and then work through the end-to-end process of launching features in that roadmap, considering all the different stakeholders and tradeoffs during the process.

In this sense, the PM interview isn't a contrived game - it's a relatively good approximation of the product manager job. So, don't just treat your interview prep as...interview prep. Treat it as preparation for the job itself!

You hopefully now understand the most basic elements of a PM interview. You know there is no guarantee on the topic you will be asked about, but there is a guarantee on the *type* of question you will be asked, and the type of skills you need to demonstrate in response. You know that above all else, you need to practice clear, structured communication and analytical thinking. You know you need to be able to take product questions about companies or products and answer them in a multidisciplinary way from high-level strategy down into specific details.

We'll now move into a deeper dive on some PM interview tips and tricks. Again, since it is hard to predict the exact question you will get asked, preparing *how* you answer is honestly far more useful than studying specific interview questions.

Afterwards, we will discuss what are arguably the four most common types of PM interview questions: behavioral, design, strategy, and analytical. It can be hard to understand how to best approach questions without understanding why the questions are being asked in the first place. So, when we describe each of these question types, we'll also talk about how they might apply to the day-to-day product management job. As we go through these tips, you'll hopefully not only gain tools to ace the PM interview, but you'll improve your thinking and communication on the whole.

Breadth before depth

Probably the biggest mistake that PM interview candidates make is trying to solve a problem too quickly. PM interview questions are extremely broad and complex. Often, you'll be asked a question that a full-time product manager may spend months trying to solve. As such, it's critical you take your time to go broad and consider the problem from many angles before you propose a solution.

For example, let's say you get asked the following interview question: "You have an unlimited budget to completely rethink the design of refrigerators. What do you build?"

A naive candidate might get nervous at how broad the question is. They'll quickly try to think of ideas, and then talk about the very first thing that comes to their mind. Perhaps they think of the idea that people hate to waste food, and so fridges could be better at helping people track the right amount of food to purchase. The candidate starts fleshing out the idea of an app that connects to the fridge, allows you to track how long each item has been in the fridge, and suggests recipes for food that is about to spoil.

On one hand, this seems like a reasonable answer. It's an interesting idea, it solves a clear problem, and perhaps the candidate was very thoughtful about how it would be built.

However, on the other hand, the candidate missed a *lot* of what the interviewer was looking for - the path to the answer is just as important as the solution itself. Why focus on reducing waste? Is that the most important issue to solve? What about other pain points such as keeping a fridge clean, it being hard to reach things in the back, different foods needing different temperatures, remembering what you have in the fridge, etc? What are the pros and cons of focusing on these different problems? Could there be a solution that tackles many of them?

The candidate would likely not get an offer because they did not demonstrate very much strategic thinking. They did not sufficiently support their proposed solution, even if the solution itself was well thought through.

As a product manager, you can't just come up with an idea and have people build it. You have to consider all the different ideas and user needs that could be addressed, and prioritize which ones matter the most.

Reducing waste is an important problem to solve, and in fact, we're sure one could make an argument that it *is* the best problem to solve. However, you must make that argument. Every answer you give should start broad - analyzing all the relevant data points, user needs, options, technologies, and more. Only narrow in on proposing a solution once you've sufficiently analyzed the problem space overall.

This will demonstrate to your interviewer that you can both think strategically and relish the details. It will highlight your analytical thinking skills, demonstrating that you can take a broad range of topics and synthesize them all into a conclusion. Finally, it will actually help you give a better answer. Forcing yourself to justify your solution before you dive into how to build it will help guarantee that your solution is valid. It will ensure that you don't forget to consider some of the critical pieces of the problem.

Finally, note that many PM interviews will not be a single cycle of broad to narrow. You may go through this cycle many times in a single interview. For instance:

1. (Broad) Start by discussing the strategic decisions facing company X

2. (Narrow) Synthesize your analysis from step #1, proposing a clear set of features you want to build

3. (Broad) Now, you go broad again, highlighting all the different things to consider when building the features you mentioned. What are all the tradeoffs and decision points?

4. (Narrow) Synthesize your analysis from #3 to build the specific flow you think is best

5. (Broad) Now, discuss different considerations for analyzing success and failure of the feature. How might success and failure be defined by different stakeholders?

6. (Narrow) Summarize which metrics and success criteria are the most important from #5

Basically, at *each step* of the problem, you want to be following this broad to narrow approach. Each phase of any answer you give should start with a structured analysis of the problem space, and only then should go a layer deeper with a proposed solution. From there, you start the process over again.

Asking for Time

The questions you'll be asked in PM interviews are open-ended and complex. As we discussed in the previous section, this is why it is critical to go broad first, rather than jumping straight into a proposed solution. However, even identifying the right areas to go broad in can be tough. It takes time to think through the different facets of a PM interview question. As such, it's critical that you take the time you need to develop a structured plan of attack.

Many candidates are afraid to ask for time to think during an interview. Silence can be uncomfortable, and you might be afraid that the interviewer expects you to answer a question right away. **Do not feel pressured to start talking right away - it is 100% okay to ask for some time to think.**

Interviewers know the questions they are asking you are complex. They would much rather see you ask for a minute to think, and then give an amazing answer, than answer right away but miss some key facets of the problem. Asking for a few minutes to think will never be held against you. Giving a poor or incomplete answer will.

We highly recommend that the first thing you say in response to every product question you are asked is: "Can I have a minute to think about that?". From there, start to figure out your plan of attack (and remember - you should start broad!). Write down the different facets of the problem you want to discuss. Once you feel like you have developed the structure with which you will approach the problem, *only then* should you start answering.

For instance, let's go back to the refrigerator question: "You have an unlimited budget to completely rethink the design of refrigerators. What do you build?". If you get asked this, start by asking for a minute to think. During that time, you might write out the following on a piece of paper or on a whiteboard:

1. Use cases for refrigerators

2. Problems with refrigerators today

3. Target customer segment

4. Tech + market trends

From here, you might tell the interviewer the following: "Alright so I would like to approach this problem in the following way. I want to start by analyzing how people use refrigerators today. From there, I want to highlight some of the pain points or issues users face today. Next, I want to briefly think through the target customers for refrigerator improvements - who drives fridge purchases? Finally, I want to discuss some of the current technological and market trends that may impact refrigerator usage (e.g. the growth of prepared meal-kit services, Internet of Things). From there, we can come up with a prioritized list of ways to redesign or re-think refrigerators. Does that seem reasonable to you?".

Look how structured and clear this response is. It delineates exactly what you are going to look into, it highlights a broad range of data points to consider before proposing a solution, and it makes it effortless for the interviewer to follow what you are saying. We would argue that unless you are the smartest person in the world, there is almost no chance you could come up with such a structured approach to solving the problem without taking a minute or two to think first.

In this sense, asking for time unlocks your potential. Having a response like the one above, rather than jumping to try to answer as quickly as possible, will make you appear ten times smarter. It enables you to calm down and make sure you're covering everything you need to in order to give a comprehensive answer to the question.

So, *ask for time*. An interviewer will never count it against you, and it will dramatically lower the chance you miss important pieces of the question.

Six magic words

No matter how well you think through a problem, if your interviewer isn't following your train of thought, you are unlikely to do well. It's your goal as the interviewee to make sure that they understand you every step of the way.

However, a lot of things can get in the way of achieving that goal. Though your interviewers may seem sage and experienced, they are fallible humans just like the rest of us. Their focus may be low because they've had a long day, they're thinking about a difficult problem pertaining to their job, or they had a bad night's sleep.

Furthermore, even if they are paying attention, they might not agree with your approach, or they may think you are missing something important. But, there is no guarantee they will tell you this on their own.

This leads us to six magical words: "Does that seem reasonable to you?".

At every logical stopping point in your answers, ask this question. Your goal is to ensure that the interviewer is following what you are saying and agrees with your approach.

A common problem that candidates face in PM interviews is they will get asked a question, and then start rambling through an answer for the entire rest of the interview without ever asking for feedback. This is a recipe for disaster. If you do this, there is a good chance the interviewer will misunderstand things you say, or will be confused by one of your conclusions. Either way, they will end up lost and you will be perceived poorly. If this happens, it's unlikely you'll get an offer.

The way you safeguard against this is by asking for feedback regularly. This is effective because it allows you to solve the confusion proactively, setting the interview back on track.

As an example, let's say you are asked an interview question, you ask for time to think, and then you lay out your plan of attack. Let's say that the interviewer doesn't quite understand what you mean for part of your plan.

If you ask "Does this seem reasonable to you?" in this situation, the interviewer is likely to bring up their confusion, and you can immediately clarify the situation. Then, you can go on with your answer, and crush the interview.

If you don't ask this, but rather just begin answering right away, the interviewer may never bring up their point of confusion. This confusion will lead to more confusion as you talk more, and will taint the interviewer's perception of the entire interview because they will never fully understand what you are saying.

The exact same person, in the exact same situation, with the exact same answer, could have polar opposite interview reviews simply based on whether they ask for feedback early on, and resolve a simple point of confusion.

So, ask for feedback! It is such a simple thing to do, but it will massively improve your interviews. You will be perceived as a much better communicator and the interviewer will be much more likely to understand all the nuances of your answers.

How often should you ask for feedback? In general, we recommend identifying natural transition points during the interview, and asking then. If you think of interviews in terms of the broad to narrow cycle we discussed earlier, these transition points often happen at the beginning and end of each broad to narrow cycle.

For example, if you get asked the refrigerator question, you might start by asking for time, outlining your high-level plan of attack, and then asking for feedback. This represents the "start" of this cycle. From there, you will discuss all the different facets to consider for redesigning a refrigerator. At some point, you will synthesize all those discussions into a conclusion. You should again ask for feedback before diving into the next phase of the answer. So, you might say something to the effect of "Based on X, Y, and Z, I want to go forward with building a refrigerator that focuses on reducing food waste. Next, I would like to dive into specific ways we could build this. Does that seem reasonable to you? ". This represents the "end" of a cycle.

Why does this process work? It ensures that you ask for feedback for each thesis you give *("I want to look at X, Y, Z to answer this question"),* and for each conclusion you provide ("Based on X and Y, I think the right next step is Z"). These are the right points to ask for feedback because they are the key elements of any analysis.

However, this process alone is not sufficient. You also want to read the facial and body cues of your interviewer. If at some point it looks like they are distracted or disengaged, that's likely a good moment to try to bring them back in by asking for feedback.

So, ask "Does this seem reasonable to you?", and make your interview a collaboration, not a monologue.

Ask for Clarification

You walk into an interview, and the interviewer asks you to improve Google search. What do you do?

If you've been paying attention so far, you'll hopefully ask for time, go broad before going narrow, and ask for feedback during your answer. However, before you do any of those things, there is something else you should do first - ask for clarification.

What exactly does it mean to improve Google search? What are you supposed to improve? There are thousands of metrics you could try to improve, and there are probably millions of ways to improve Google Search (you could improve it for a certain geography, for a certain type of search, for a certain type of content, etc.).

It's important to clarify these questions so that you and the interviewer are on the same page about what the goals of the interview are. This is especially true for product manager interviews given how broad the questions can be. If you don't clarify, you may answer the question in a totally different way from what the interviewer intends. In this case, even if you provide a well thought out answer, you may not get rated very well.

If your interviewer asks you to design a better refrigerator, you might start by asking what type of refrigerator they are talking about. Are you trying to improve industrial and kitchen grade refrigerators, or the typical refrigerator you see in people's homes?

Once you have clarified the question, then you can dive into asking for time and doing all the other things we mentioned. But, your first step should always be to clarify.

—

We've now highlighted a number of key tips for approaching PM interviews. You hopefully have a very good sense of what a PM interview is like, the characteristics you need to demonstrate in your answers, and some simple heuristics you can utilize to ensure you answer questions well.

From here, we'll break PM questions down into their four major categories: behavioral, product design, strategy, and analytical. For each, we'll give some specific tips about how to answer that type of question, and provide a sample interview scripts as well.

Behavioral Questions

In our experience, there are two main types of behavioral questions that you may encounter:

1. General questions you would expect at any interview - For example: "Why do you want to be in this company/role?", "What are you uniquely good at?", "Tell me about yourself."

2. Tell me about a time... - For example: "Tell me about a time you dealt with a difficult person?", "What's a time where you influenced someone you didn't have authority over?"

Both of these question types are common at virtually *all* jobs you might apply for out of college, and there are plenty of resources out there that cover how to answer these questions in depth. As such, we won't spend too much time talking through advice for these - we'll focus on the highlights. If you want more help, a simple google search will give you more advice than you could ever read.

For the first type of question, you simply want to make sure you have a very strong answer for:

1.   Why you are interested in the company

2.   Why you are interested in the role

3.   Your background, personality, and characteristics

Make sure you've done your research about the company you are applying to and understand its products, culture, leadership, and mission well. Additionally, make sure you understand the scope of the job (hopefully this book has helped you with that). Finally, make sure you have done a good amount of introspection, and have a clear story about who you are and where you want to go in life.

If you do the above, you'll be covered for the first type of behavioral question. This shouldn't require very much preparation time at all.

For the second type of behavioral question ("Tell me about a time where you did XYZ"), you should make sure you have 3-6 good stories from your past that somehow deal with failure, challenges, teamwork, leadership, entrepreneurship, or similar skills that are valuable as a PM.

For example, if there was a time in a past internship where you convinced your manager to make a decision by going out of your way to run a user study and collect metrics, that might show how you can be data-driven, entrepreneurial, and influence without authority.

Similarly, maybe there was a time where you had a team project in class and one of your teammates was extremely difficult to work with and jeopardized the success of the project, but you worked with the person to overcome these issues. This would be a great way to demonstrate communication, leadership, and ability to resolve issues between teams or people.

If you get asked these questions in a PM interview, the questions will likely focus on a skill that PMs should be adept at. So, we recommend thinking about your experiences primarily in the context of the product management skills we outlined earlier in the book: leadership, communication, product strategy and design, analytical thinking, and technical skills. Just like you want your resume to touch on the PM skillset, you want the stories you tell in interviews to revolve around the PM skill-set.

If you have followed our advice about preparing for a PM job while in college, you should hopefully have a wealth of experiences to talk about since you have already oriented your classes, extracurriculars, and personal projects around these skills.

However, just having the experiences is not enough - you need to be able to communicate them well to an interviewer. Practice telling each experience to yourself, picking out a specific skill to frame the story around. For instance, tell the story of your internship project as if someone asked you about a time you demonstrated product sense. Don't skip over details - walk the interviewer through exactly what happened, your mindset and decision process at each step, and the detailed manner in which your work demonstrated the given skill.

A good aid for behavioral interviews can be creating a behavioral experiences list like the one below, which summarizes each experience, and the traits it maps to.

Experience	Traits Exhibited
Started a new club and convinced school to fund it. Grew it to 15 active members.	Leadership, Communication and Sales, Entrepreneurial
Started a small business at school doing food delivery to campus. Built website + marketed service. Growing to 10,000 in revenue/year.	Product strategy + design, leadership, analytical thinking
While working as a software engineering intern at a startup, pulled user metrics to convince manager to go a different way with a product	Data-driven, entrepreneurial

decision.	
Was working on feature during my internship where two leaders had really different opinions on the way it should be built. Took initiative to understand each side's constraints, identify an ideal middle ground, and present a proposal to align everyone.	Communication, leadership, product sense, creativity, resolve conflict
Did advertising design (flyers, facebook ads, etc) for 15+ clubs on campus.	Product design, entrepreneurial
Took Udemy machine learning course. Created a sample photo labeling ML app.	Technical skills

We highly recommend writing up a document similar to this with your own experiences. It will ensure you are prepared for any behavioral questions if they come your way.

Product Design Questions

Design questions are the most common and, for many, the most difficult questions that you will encounter in a PM interview. However, if you are a good fit for the job and learn how to think through these questions, they can also be the most fun! A product design interview should be more of a dialogue and exchange of ideas between the interviewee and interviewer than anything else. You should treat it as an interesting problem to brainstorm.

The most typical product design question you'll get is *how would you design x for y?* (or, more broadly, *how would you design X in Y way*). This may involve a tech product, or it may not. Here are a few examples of what we mean:

1. Design a news app that is based entirely on video, rather than text

2. Let's say you could completely rethink and redesign the vending machine. What would you build?

3. Walk me through how you could redesign the security and boarding experiences in an airport

As we've tried to emphasize, and as these examples demonstrate, the range of things you can be asked about is massive. Furthermore, these questions are quite broad and don't really have a "right" answer. As such, the first thing to keep in mind is the set of tips we mentioned earlier in this chapter: ask for clarification, go broad before going deep, don't be afraid to ask for time, and make sure you're checking in with the interviewer. Furthermore, above all else, focus on clear communication and structured answers.

Let's consider the interview question "*Design a refrigerator for the elderly*".

Spend 5-10 minutes right now thinking through how you would approach this question. What key things would you consider? What sub-problems would you split it into? How would you avoid rambling, and instead present a cohesive and easy to follow answer? We'll guide you through how we might approach it below, but it is worthwhile to try it on your own first to really practice, and to then compare how you answered to our answer (and who knows - your answer may even be better!).

Done? Great - now we'll walk you through our response.

Asking for clarification

Like most questions, we would begin by asking for clarification to ensure we fully understand what is being asked. This will help us better understand what we are trying to optimize for, and what we *don't* need to worry about. It will ensure the interviewer and us are on the same page from the beginning.

> **Interviewer:** I want you to tell me how you'd think through designing a refrigerator for old people.
>
> **Candidate:** Sounds good. I just wanted to understand a few things before jumping into the design.
>
> **Interviewer:** Sure, happy to answer any questions.
>
> **Candidate:** Great! Who are the purchasers of the refrigerators? Will the elderly person be living by themselves or with a caretaker?

Interviewer: Let's assume that you're designing for elderly people who live alone.

Candidate: Sounds good. I'm assuming that I'm the manufacturer of these refrigerators. What am I optimizing for in particular? Do I need to consider cost or other physical constraints in terms of building the refrigerator?

Interviewer: You're trying to create an ideal user experience for the elderly. Cost isn't a huge consideration, but you should be able to create a refrigerator in the same price range as a normal feature.

Candidate: Great, that makes sense. So it sounds like I'm creating a fridge under normal budget constraints and trying to optimize for delivering an amazing user experience for elderly people living alone? Does that sound reasonable to you?

Interviewer: Yep! Let's jump into the design.

Listing Out Users Needs and Pain Points

Now that we understand the question well, we need to figure out our strategy for answering it. Central to this is developing a good outline of the unique needs of our users (in this case the elderly), and what that means in terms of designing a refrigerator for them. In other words, we want to spend some time defining two key things:

1. What is the purpose of a refrigerator?
2. What characteristics of elderly users might impact the way a refrigerator needs to be designed for them?

We'll synthesize this all together to explain the "pain points" that the elderly might have with a refrigerator's typical functions. From there, we'll be able to propose solutions.

Remember, being extremely user focused is critical when engaging in this type of thinking. If you ever face questions like this, try to think of people in your life who would be a good archetype for the user you're trying to help. Or, try to pretend you are that user yourself. You need to really dive deep on what makes your target user different from the "average" person.

> **Candidate:** I'd like to start by listing out the different ways people use refrigerators. From there, I want to define some of the unique characteristics of the elderly, and highlight which refrigerator use cases might therefore pose problems to them.

> **Interviewer:** That seems like a good place to begin.

> **Candidate:** To start, at the highest level, the purpose of a refrigerator is to store food which otherwise is perishable. Given this, there are a number of high level ways people use refrigerators to achieve this purpose:
>
> 1. Putting new food in.
> 2. Taking food out. There are a few reasons this can happen, such as it going bad, or planning to cook with it, or cleaning it.
> 3. Organizing and re-arranging food to make it easy to find things.
> 4. Using the water and ice area to get a drink.

It is also worth noting that most refrigerators have two key compartments: a freezer area, and a regular fridge area.

Now, when I think of the unique problems faced by elderly users, a few things immediately come to mind. First, the elderly typically have issues with dexterity and strength. For instance, my Grandma has trouble reaching items at the back of the fridge and putting heavier groceries in and out of the fridge. This could also make cleaning much more complicated - as that often involves taking *everything* out of the fridge and then putting it all back in. The elderly are also likely more susceptible to extreme temperatures, and so I would imagine that opening the fridge and getting that cold gust of wind isn't a very pleasant experience for them. Lastly, I think for many elderly folks memory is an issue. So they might not remember things like when certain items are going bad, where they put the milk, etc. They may not even remember if they have a certain item in their fridge or freezer.

So, to recap, I think it could be worthwhile to dive deeper into the following problems: the **physical and mobility issues** elderly may face around putting groceries in and out of the fridge, the **user experience issues** around extra sensitivity to cold, and the **memory issues** around knowing what is in the fridge and what isn't, and when it may go bad.

I think these are all problems worth solving.

Choosing a Pain Point to Solve

In any design interview, you will eventually reach the point where you have completed an initial analysis of the problem space, and highlighted some key areas that you could pursue further. It is at this point where you will need to focus on *prioritization* - where should you start, and what should you focus on?

You will never have time to fully cover everything in a 45 minute interview. This mirrors the fact that there will always be more ideas than your team has time to address when you are working as a product manager. So, you need to figure out what will have the biggest impact.

Analyze the tradeoffs inherent in each paint point or user need which you could solve. Which would represent the biggest improvement for users if solved? Which have feasible solutions or low cost solutions? Present a logical argument that justifies taking a certain path, and *not taking* the others.

> **Interviewer:** Those are all interesting problems. Which do you think is the most important to solve?
>
> **Candidate:** I think the mobility issue is the most important problem to solve. First, it is the most fundamental usability issue - if you can't even properly load and unload groceries, then it is irrelevant whether or not you can remember what is in the fridge. This is particularly true since we are discussing elderly who live alone, and therefore won't have physical help available all the time. Second, it is a safety issue. If an elderly person isn't able to reach an item or tries to lift something that is too heavy, they might hurt themselves in the process. Third, while there are other tools that could help with some of the other problems

mentioned (notes and grocery tracking apps for memory, warmer clothes and additional layers), I can't think of many alternative solutions that exist for the mobility problem.

Given this, I'm going to focus on designing a fridge that makes it easier for people with limited strength and mobility to put in and retrieve items from their fridge. Does that seem reasonable to you?

Interviewer: Sounds good.

Brainstorming Solutions

Once you have agreed on the problem to solve, it is time to brainstorm ways to solve it. When doing this, try to be as creative as possible. Don't limit yourself by worrying if an idea might be a little too ridiculous or out there. Even if an idea is kind of crazy, talking through it and considering it will often give you additional insights, or outside the box thoughts, which will ultimately drive you to a better answer overall.

You can always filter out bad ideas later. But, if you don't let your creativity run wild at first, you will end up with bland and boring answers. If you are worried an interviewer might think an idea is stupid, you can hedge your language a little when introducing it to clarify that you recognize there are downsides. For instance - "One kind of out there idea is to do X. While this may cause problems given Y, there may be ways to address that. We can revisit this a little later."

Another key tip is to think very carefully about "assumptions" built into the product today. Why is the product typically designed in X way? Does it need to be? That line of thinking will often lead to novel insights, or interesting alternative ways to help solve the user's needs.

Finally, remember to ask for time if you need it! Coming up with ideas can be challenging, so give yourself the time you need to do it well.

> **Candidate:** Is it alright if I spend some time thinking about how to do this?

> **Interviewer:** Sure, take your time.

> **Candidate:** [1-2 minutes pass as candidate writes some ideas down on a notepad] Okay - so when I think about mobility with fridges, there are a few movement patterns which could be problematic. The first is the need to reach something very far back inside the fridge. The second is the need to put something very high or very low, requiring either excessive reaching or bending. I think different types of designs could address each of these problems.

> Starting with the first one, I think one issue with the current design of refrigerators is that it's really hard for the elderly to reach items near the back of the fridge, or put items in the back. Reaching so far in puts you off balance, and if you're holding something heavy, it can put a lot of torque on your body. A lot of these issues are a consequence of the structure of the shelves - refrigerator shelves today are flat and immobile. I wonder if the shelves inside the fridge could be circular and spin like dollies so that there isn't a concept of front vs. back.

Interviewer: If the shelves were circular, wouldn't that cause some potential other issues to consider?

Candidate: The primary issue I see is that fridges are rectangular (and homes and apartments are designed for rectangular fridges). As a result, if there is a circular shelf, there may be spaces where items could fall down in the corners. However, you could have more conventional ledges in the fridge on each corner, with just the center circle able to rotate. This would leave no gaps, but would still enable the majority of the fridge to support rotation.

Interviewer: That's an interesting idea. Do you have any others?

Candidate: An alternative way to address this problem would be for the ledges to somehow extend in and out. For example - imagine I could press a button for a shelf, and that shelf could extend out of the fridge. This would make it much easier for me to put things on the back of that shelf. I could then press the button again for the shelf to retract.

Both of the solutions mentioned so far would involve some degree of additional complexity in terms of mechanical and electric elements in the fridge, but I don't think either would be excessively complicated. Another downside of these solutions is that they would make the fridge far less "composable" - most fridges today allow you to rearrange shelves, or take them in and out, to create space for bigger items. However, for the elderly population we are focusing on, this seems like an acceptable tradeoff.

Now, I'd like to spend some time exploring the second mobility issue I mentioned: having to reach high and low. First, this actually seems like the bigger problem to me. Bending over or reaching up very high on your tip-toes while lifting something heavy puts you at a much greater risk of injury than just reaching far back on a shelf.

One way to potentially address this would be to extend the concept of shelves that can come in and out, and have a shelf that can come out and then move up and down. Need to put something on a bottom shelf? That shelf can move out, then move up to the height of the user's torso. Once the item is put onto it, the user can press a button for it to move back. This would ensure an elderly person can always interact with a shelf as if it were at the height of their torso.

An additional benefit of this type of design is it would make putting heavy items into the fridge much simpler. If this shelf could also lower down near the floor, the user could simply drop the heavy item onto it, rather than ever having to lift it up themselves. In this sense, the design could act similarly to a forklift.

An alternative approach with similar benefits would be for the fridge shelves to be designed more like a "ferris wheel", where the shelves can all rotate around and ultimately be presented right in front of the user. However, this may be much more complex mechanically and would likely make it harder to fully utilize all the space in the fridge.

Choosing a Solution

Once you've brainstormed several possible ideas, it is time to finally start filtering them down until only the best remain. When you do this, you'll want to take a holistic approach. Consider all of the different factors you can think of - cost, engineering effort, complexity, impact of the solution, second order effects the solution might have, etc - in order to identify the best solutions.

> **Interviewer:** These are some interesting ideas. Let's say you are prioritizing for your team, and you need to pick one to actually prototype and build. Which would you implement first?

> **Candidate:** While the ideas that revolve around shelves that can go in and out or otherwise move electronically have some nice potential benefits, they would also be quite complicated to build. They would also be substantial departures from the way that refrigerators are built today. I suspect this may cause problems from the perspective of manufacturing, and it may introduce many more ways for a refrigerator to fail or break. This is especially a problem given that we are targeting an older population - if something breaks, they may have an especially hard time understanding how to fix it.

> As such, I think the right starting point is the simpler approach of having the shelves better support rotation. While this does not

solve every single problem, I think it is a lower cost, lower risk solution that clearly addresses a need among elderly people.

I would likely start with that solution, and then test and validate to see if our hypotheses are correct. Does that seem reasonable to you?

Interviewer: Sounds good!

Implementation and Success Metrics

You've now reached the point where the interview is likely to get a lot more detailed. You have theorized a lot about user needs and paint points, brainstormed solutions, and come up with a logical framework for moving forward with one of them. Now, you need to actually design your solution.

Expect to be asked about many minute details of your proposal. You should be ready to articulate exactly how it will work and look, and you should anticipate edge cases or usability problems that your solution might introduce.

At this stage of the interview, it is often useful to use the whiteboard to sketch out exactly what you're thinking. After you sketch out your design, you should be able to talk about how you would test the success (or failure) of your product.

emphasize testing

Interviewer: Tell me more about exactly what this design would look like.

Candidate: So I am imagining that each shelf would be a combination of two pieces. There would be a flat base with a circular indentation in the middle, and an even deeper circular indentation in the center, and then there would be a circular disk. The circular disk can be placed within the indentation of the base, allowing it to freely rotate, and creating a final surface which is "flat" on top (goes to whiteboard and draws picture of design).

Cross Section of Shelf

Top-Down View of Shelf

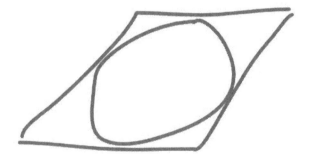

In effect, the shelf design would be similar to that of a microwave. This would be a very simple mechanism, which still allows shelves to easily be rearranged or taken out, but which enables the *majority* of each shelf to rotate (only the corners would not be able to). These shelves could be manually rotated, similar to a lazy susan, removing the need for wiring or electronics attached to each shelf.

In addition to the above, we may want to limit the height of the refrigerator, in order to ensure that there is little risk of something falling on top of an elderly person.

I need to figure out how to do this gracefully

Finally, one other idea I forgot to mention earlier was that refrigerator doors can be extremely hard to open, which could pose a major problem for an elderly person. I might consider altering the door design for this refrigerator as well. One approach would be for the door to have a latch which allows it to open and close, rather than just relying on pressure. Another idea would be to allow the door to slide to the side.

Interviewer: The door being hard to open is a good point, but let's focus on the shelf redesign. Are there any potential downsides to this design?

Candidate: We would need to consider whether having excessive food on one side of a circular disk, but not the other, might cause it to lean or tilt in a way that makes it difficult to rotate.

I would also want to test whether elderly people can easily rotate the circular shelves manually. If not, we could consider additional ways to make it easier to rotate, such as elevating the circular piece a little bit or adding small handles or grips that make it easier to rotate.

There is a chance that some people will be confused by the fact that part of each shelf can rotate, but not all of the shelf. This is something that user testing could help us better evaluate.

Finally, shelves like this comprised of multiple layers would likely need to be much thicker than regular fridge shelves. This would theoretically reduce the maximum amount of available space in a refrigerator - either there would need to be fewer shelves per unit of vertical height, or there would need to be less vertical space between each shelf. This would reduce the amount that one can store either way. However, I think this is a reasonable tradeoff. On average, I would guess that an elderly person living alone would have fewer items in their fridge than the average household. So, I don't think total usable volume is an important metric to this type of user. We would definitely want to validate this by talking to users though.

Interviewer: Sure makes sense. So let's assume that you implemented this design, how would you determine success?

Candidate: Ideally, we could quickly prototype this fridge before committing to manufacturing thousands of them. It would be pretty easy to make a few makeshift versions of this type of shelf, and then go install them into existing refrigerators. This is a key benefit of this proposed solution - the shelves could theoretically be sold individually and retrofitted onto existing refrigerators, rather than requiring the manufacturing of brand new refrigerators.

Given this, we could do a trial run with a set of elderly people living by themselves. I would start by observing them as I ask them to do a few specific tasks with our shelves, such as putting items in, taking them out, rotating the shelves and more. This would allow me to understand if the elderly can mechanically utilize the shelf, as well as whether they any value in the design.

I would then have them keep a journal in the kitchen, use the fridge for a few weeks, and write notes each time they use it. This log of notes would help me better understand if they actually *use* the shelves in their normal day-to-day lives, and if any unexpected problems come up after a longer period of use. At the end of the test period, I would probe the users on whether they would want to continue to use this refrigerator, and whether they would recommend it to others.

specific + later feedback [handwritten margin note]

If we had a few more resources and wanted to gather more quantitative feedback, we could install small sensors on our makeshift test shelves which track rotation. This would allow us to measure things like how often people are spinning the shelf. This is likely the most important "engagement" metric for this product. *He brings up metrics too* [handwritten note]

As a next step, you could run a longer term longitudinal study with these refrigerators, comparing the injury rate among elderly people who use them vs. those who use use a typical refrigerator. This could possibly provide very compelling data around the enhanced safety of the product.

Finally, once we fully launch the product, I would want to look at metrics like sales figures specifically among the elderly population.

While this is just one sample design question, we hope it gives you some insight into how these questions are typically structured. This pattern of identifying user needs, prioritizing a need, brainstorming solutions, prioritizing solutions, designing a solution, and then identifying success for that solution is extremely common. While the things you consider will be vastly different depending on the product you are asked about, the thought processes and approach you should take are generally the same.

So, every few days, spend 15 minutes thinking about how you would design something. It could be an app you love to use, a website you hate to use, or an interesting new idea for an emerging technology. To make it harder, add some constraints on the problem, such as focusing on a certain type of user, or limiting yourself to only certain options (e.g. Could you build a useful budgeting app that doesn't have direct access to your bank account? What would that look like?).

Forcing yourself into this type of thinking regularly will help you more than you can imagine with interviews. It's all about practicing the mindset and thought process. It can seem overwhelming to answer questions like this at first, but over time you will get much better at it.

Before we dive into the next type of interview question, here are a few additional examples of product design questions that might be fun to answer:

1. Walk me through how the design of the Uber app would change, assuming that Uber has a fleet of self driving cars.

2. Assume that Robinhood decides that it needs to help its users better understand the investments they are making, and the risks associated with them. How might you redesign the app to improve user education around risky investments (e.g. individual stocks, cryptocurrencies)?

3. Design a voice-navigation only phone. Assuming voice recognition were sufficiently advanced, would this ever be the ideal experience for a user, or for certain types of users?

4. It's common practice for companies to have some sort of "master" brand slide deck with a bunch of template slides styled for the company. Employees are encouraged to use these to create their slide decks to ensure consistency in company presentations. What problems can arise from this sort of workflow today, and what kinds of tools or features could be built to improve these problems?

5. Let's say you are a PM at Spotify and you see that many users are switching to Apple Music. What types of features could you build to help make Spotify more "sticky" for such users?

6. What are the 4 most critical features that Slack needed to focus on to go from attracting small teams to signing major corporate contracts? Explain why and fully design one.

Strategy Questions

As a product manager, your job is not just to figure out the right way to design a solution to a given user need. You also need to determine which user needs and problems you care about solving.

For example, an interesting design question would be to map out how Airbnb's product would change if it allowed hotels to list rooms just like people can list their homes. However, no Airbnb product manager would ever spend time answering that question without first determining if such a decision were strategically correct. Answering *that* has little to do with the details and minutiae of product design. Instead, it involves having a deep understanding of all the players involved - end users, airbnb hosts, hotels, other travel booking sites - and the dynamics between them. It involves answering questions like:

- Could this allow Airbnb to become more of a centralized platform for all types of travel? What might the business impact of that be?
- Would this dilute the Airbnb brand for users? How would existing Airbnb users respond to this?
- What are the incentive structures for hotels to want to, or not want to, do this?
- How much work would this be to do? What would you *not* be doing as a result?

Being good at this type of high level strategic thinking is critical because it is what ultimately drives a product roadmap. It is only after you have defined a clear roadmap that you can start to get down into the details of designing, iterating on, testing, and launching features.

For this reason, it is very common to be asked strategy questions during PM interviews. Here are a few other examples:

1. Why did Google build Android or Chrome? Why not just stick with their core search + advertising strategy?
2. Why has Uber invested so much money in a self driving car division?
3. Why does Netflix invest billions of dollars a year into producing content?
4. How do you bootstrap a marketplace business?
5. What are the top 3 things the board of directors of Twilio is likely discussing each month?
6. Why did Amazon acquire Twitch?
7. Is Tesla's position in the electric car market actually defensible, or will other brands (BMW, Volvo, etc) quickly catch up?

You'll note that these questions are just as varied, if not even more so, than product design questions. Not only can you get asked about almost any company (though these questions will likely center on the industries or areas of the company you are applying to), but you can get asked about everything from acquisitions to strategic decisions, technology trends, and broader changes in the world and the opportunities or risks they pose.

As such, once again, it is going to be almost impossible to directly anticipate or prepare for the specific strategy questions you will get asked. Instead, you need to develop your general skillset around analytical thinking and structured communication to respond effectively to this type of question. Rather than focusing on aspects of user psychology, visual and interaction design, metrics and instrumentation, and defining user journeys through the product, you'll be thinking about business models, technological trends, incentive structures, and the way that marketing, sales, and positioning impact product decisions.

To go through a complete example, let's consider the interview question *"Why has Uber invested so much money in a self driving car division?"*.

Once again, spend some time trying to answer this on your own right now. Remember the overall tips we mentioned before - those all still apply!

—

Done? Alright - here's how we might approach it. This time we'll go all the way through, and then highlight some key takeaways afterwards.

> **Interviewer:** Why has Uber invested so much money in a self driving car division? Is this a smart decision by them?

> **Candidate:** Can you give me a few minutes to think through that?

> **Interviewer:** Sure (2 minutes pass)

> **Candidate:** So, ultimately, I think this question revolves around what the competitive dynamics will be in a world where self driving cars exist. If we can map that out, we can see where Uber fits in, and how having invested into self driving car tech would play a role. So, I'd like to start by mapping out what the

transportation industry might look like in that world. Does that sound reasonable?

Interviewer: Sounds good to me

Candidate: Great. Okay so to start, let's assume we are in a world where fully autonomous self driving cars exist. What will the different layers of the transportation stack look like? Roughly, I think you can divide it into the following pieces:

1. The companies who manufacture the physical components. E.g. doors, the frame, lights, sensors.
2. The companies who provide the "Operating System" of the car. This might be split into regular software functions (e.g. music player) and the self-driving algorithms.
3. The companies who provide the platform to order a self driving car (the user entrypoint).

Today, car manufacturers (e.g. Toyota) do #1, car manufacturers also do #2 (for the most part), and Uber/Lyft do #3. How might this change once self driving cars arrive?

Ultimately, I think the most defensible piece of this chain will be the self driving car algorithm layer. There are a few reasons for this. The first is that the complexity and difficulty of producing a robust self driving car algorithm is enormous, and requires insane amounts of data and engineering prowess. Only a few companies can realistically do this.

Secondly, the self driving car algorithm will have very powerful network effects. People are going to be very nervous about the safety of self driving cars, and so are going to gravitate towards the service which has the best (and therefore safest) algorithms. This will in turn give that company more data, which will allow it to further improve its models, making it safer. This will then draw even more users, and the cycle will repeat.

In contrast, manufacturing will be totally commoditized (most manufacturing is already commoditized today).

While the user entrypoint is also valuable, I suspect it is less critical. The company with the best self driving algorithms could likely launch its own ride hailing service (especially if it is Google and it can leverage Maps) and easily draw users away from Lyft or Uber.

So, what does this mean for Uber? Well, if they don't end up owning the self driving software piece, then I suspect whichever company does will launch a competitor ride-hailing app and totally beat out Uber. As such, it is critical for Uber to try to be the company to own the self driving software, as this is the only way to prevent that from happening.

Given this, I would tend to lean towards this being a smart decision by Uber, as in the long run they depend on it.

Interviewer: And to play devil's advocate, what would be the counter argument to what you just said? Why should Uber *not* invest in self driving technology?

Candidate: I think there are a few assumptions I made earlier which I could be wrong about.

First, it's possible that the ride-hailing piece is more defensible than I am suggesting. Let's say Uber ends up becoming the de-facto transportation app (which it looks like they are trying to be given their recent pushes into transit directions). In other words, it becomes the default place for users to go when looking to transport themselves.

It's possible that it owns this space so completely that it becomes hard, if not impossible, for another company to launch a competitive ride hailing service. In that world, the self driving software companies would be forced to license their software to Uber, and Uber would have a lot more relative power.

Another possibility would be that I am over-exaggerating the defensibility of self driving software. Perhaps the data network effects are not actually going to be that strong, and a number of companies all develop reasonably good software which isn't very differentiated to users. In this world, the self driving software becomes a commodity, and the ride-hailing piece is the key thing to own.

If either of those things were true, Uber would be better off not wasting money and time trying to develop the self driving software, and should just keep trying to become the place for transportation.

(Was your answer even better? We hope so!)

This sample answer highlights a few really important factors to keep in mind for strategy questions.

First, note how we did not start by trying to directly answer the question. In fact, we did not really address the question until the end of our analysis - we spent the vast majority of our answer on the transportation industry in general. The reason for this is that, just like design questions, there is generally not a "right" answer to strategy questions. What matters is how you arrive at an answer, not the answer itself.

As such, start by articulating the different elements related to the problem, and the ways they relate. Highlight how you want to approach answering the question. Touch on the key things you think are relevant, and then spend some time thinking through each of them.

If you do this methodically, by the end of your response you will have developed a good answer to the question, even if you had no clue what to say when it was first asked. This is a key principle, because for a huge portion of strategy questions you will have never thought about it before, and therefore you will not have an opinion ready. Don't freeze in this situation, just start to list out the key facets and reason through them. You will eventually arrive at a good answer.

Second, note how we incorporated a few points about recent trends in the tech industry, such as Uber moving into public transit, and Google's advancements with Waymo and their likelihood to leverage Google Maps. Slipping a few comments like this into strategy answers will make you seem more intelligent and add depth and sophistication to your answer.

Third, notice the structure we maintained throughout the response. We always made it very clear how we were going to answer the question, and we walked the interviewer through our logic and rationale step by step. When you are asked these broad strategy questions, it is absolutely critical to do this.

Please, please, please do not answer a question like this in the following manner: "Well, self driving will probably be a big deal and change a lot of things. So, companies should be investing money into it so they can try to be the one who does self driving. And Uber is already in the transportation industry, so it probably makes sense for them to do it."

There is absolutely no analysis in a response like that. You are just repeating a few surface level facts. *You need to drill deeper*. The way to do that is to more thoroughly outline the companies, trends, technologies, user behaviors, and other entities that relate to the question, and then talk through each in a structured way.

For a question like this, immediately the following questions should be shooting through your mind as key things to outline during the interview:

1. What does Uber do today? Who are their competitors?
2. What is the state of self driving technology? Who is working on it? What are these companies good at?
3. Once self driving cars become commonplace, what will the end to end experience look like for getting a car?
4. What will users care about in a self driving car world?

If you start by listing out questions like this in your head, you can demarcate the key areas you need to explore and think through. Once you have those, you have the key to answering the question - it's just a matter of time at that point.

One additional tip for strategy questions is to spend some time researching a few basic things about any company you are interviewing with. This research will often lay the groundwork for an answer to any strategy questions you get asked. Good research questions include:

1. Why is this company successful? Assuming infinite resources, what would prevent another companies from copying the product or easily stealing market share?
2. What are all this company's product lines? Why has the company pursued all of these things, rather than just focusing on some? What synergies exist between them?
3. What are the biggest competitive threats to the company? Why?
4. What is the company's business model? How do they make money (or do they not make money)? Why have they chosen to monetize in this way (or not at all)?
5. What assumptions about the future is this company depending on? What would lead those assumptions to be incorrect?

Finally, here are a few additional strategy question examples to go through on your own:

1. What led Snapchat to grow so rapidly at first? Why is it struggling so much now?
2. Why has it been so hard for modern technology companies to disrupt electronic health records companies like Epic, even though such a high percentage of doctors and nurses dislike the product?

3. What are the biggest threats to Apple?

4. Why is Amazon launching a series of physical bookstores?

5. Are decentralized social networks actually a threat to Facebook?

Now that you have seen these examples and have a stronger sense of the purpose of strategy questions, it should hopefully be pretty easy to come up with your own as well.

Analytical Questions

Analytical questions are meant to test whether or not you can approach problems from a quantitative and mathematical perspective. In our experience, most PM analytical questions fall into one of two camps:

- **Estimation** - Estimating some value by breaking a nebulous problem down into pieces, identifying corner cases, and using intuition and gut to check whether you're in the right ballpark.

  e.g. "Estimate how many messages are sent on Slack each day"

- **Metrics and Analytics** - Answering a series of questions about how you would measure certain things for a product, and how you would interpret certain numbers.

  e.g. "What core metrics would you look at as a PM of slack? Why? Let's say you launch a feature that changes metric X in this way but metric Y in this way - what does that imply?"

Since these questions need to be handled somewhat differently, we'll go through each one independently.

Estimation Questions

In our experience, estimation or market sizing questions don't typically have much bearing on your day to day life as a product manager. But, for whatever reason, companies really like to ask them. So, we want to help you prepare for them!

The most important thing to know about these questions is that they are *not* meant to measure general knowledge about any specific domain or test how close you can get to the answer. They are really only about the path you take to reach an answer; how do you reason through an ambiguous, open ended question?

A rough framework you might use for this kind of question is:

- **Clarify**

- **Break it Down**

- **Calculate**

- **Check**

Let's walk through the following market sizing question: *"Estimate the number of hours people in the US spend streaming Netflix every year"*.

Clarify

Like you should be doing for all interview questions, start by ensuring that you're clear on the exact parameters of the question.

Interviewer: So I want you to estimate the total number of hours users in the United States spend watching Netflix every year.

Candidate: Great - so just to clarify, we are talking about how much time people spend watching Netflix and if two users are watching one device for an hour, that still counts as two hours?

Interviewer: Yes - it is total time spent for all users, not all devices.

Break it Down

The next step is to break down the large question into smaller pieces. Basically, you want to come up with a high-level equation for how to estimate your end-goal. The equation doesn't have to be exact, but it should demonstrate that you are taking into account the important high-level variables.

Candidate: To get to an estimate, I want to find the product of how many Netflix users there are in the United States and how many hours each of those users watch Netflix every year. Does that seem reasonable to you?

Written on the whiteboard: # of Netflix users in United States x hours each user watches in a year

Interviewer: That seems like a reasonable place to start.

Candidate: Great, so to find the number of Netflix users in the United States, I'll want to break that down into the number of people in the United States multiplied by the percentage of people who are in Netflix's target age demographic multiplied by the percentage of people in the target demographic that have a Netflix account.

Written on the whiteboard: (# people in the US x % of people in Netflix age demographic x % of people in demographic who are Netflix users) x hours each user watches in a year

Interviewer: Okay that seems like an alright way to approach the number of Netflix users. How do you think you would get the number of hours each user watches in a year?

Candidate: I would probably extrapolate out from how many hours a user is likely to watch a week. I would then multiply that by the number of weeks in a year.

Written on the whiteboard: (# people in the US x % of people in Netflix age demographic x % of people in demographic who are Netflix users) x (hours each user watches per week x number of weeks in a year)

Interviewer: Sounds reasonable to me.

Calculate

Now that you have a high-level formula, you want to start putting ballpark numbers next to those formulas. For most components in the formula, you can't and won't get the exact number correct; that's okay. The important part is to show common sense when estimating and to make sure you talk about the assumptions you are making.

Candidate: Based on what I've seen from friends and family, the average amount of time I'd expect a Netflix user to watch Netflix per week is around 5 hours. That'll account for 30 minutes per day on weekdays and a little more than an hour each weekend day. We'll want to multiply that by 52 to get to the number of hours we expect a user to watch every year. I'll just make that a round 50 to make the calculation simpler. So, that leads to about 250 hours a year per user.

Written on the whiteboard: (# people in the US x % of people in Netflix age demographic x % of people in demographic who are Netflix users) x 250

Interviewer: Do you think you and your friends are the typical Netflix user?

Candidate: I would *guess* it is the most common case, but there are likely other segments of users. I can think of 3 high level categories: people with tons of free time who binge watch a lot (e.g. college students), people with a typical work life but who are generally engaged, and people who subscribe but barely watch at all.

Let's say the first group is around 20% of users, and watches *much* more, watching maybe an hour a day during the week and possibly binging a few episodes each weekend, coming out to around 5 hours during the week, and maybe 5 more on the weekend, leading to 10 total.

The second group is likely the majority of users, let's say 60%, and I think falls under the estimate I made earlier of about 5 hours a week.

The third group might only watch every second or third week, and just watch maybe one hour or so each time. This brings them to not much more than 30 minutes a week on average.

If you average this together, you would end up with:

Written on the whiteboard: (.2 * 10) + (.6 * 5) + (.2 * .5) ~ 2 + 3 + .1 ~ 5 hours a week

So, in the end, we end up with roughly the same average across all users.

Interviewer: Okay, sounds good.

Candidate: Now let's move onto the other portion of the equation.

Now I know that there are about 300 million people in the United States and I would assume that almost all Netflix users are between 15-55. Most young people aren't in control of household purchasing behavior and might have restrictions on what/how much they can watch, and most older people are less likely to be technology adopters. Since the average life expectancy in the US is about 80 and 15-55 is a 40 year range, I'll assume 50% of users fit into the possible demographic. Does that seem reasonable?

Written on the whiteboard: (# people in the US (300 mill) x %
of people in Netflix age demographic (50%) x % of people in
demographic who are Netflix users) x 250

Interviewer: Sure.

Candidate: I think anecdotally, about a third to a half of my friends and family are Netflix users. But it's also worth noting that most of the people I know are middle to upper class. Netflix is an extraneous expense, so I expect some households might not want to pay for it. To take this into account, I'll estimate on the lower side - that 20% of people in the age demographic are actual users. Does that seem reasonable?

Written on the whiteboard: (# people in the US (300 mill) x % of people in Netflix age demographic (50%) x % of people in demographic who are Netflix users (20%)) x 250

Interviewer: Great, so what's the total number of hours you'd estimate?

Candidate: *(Does whiteboard calculations)* So it looks like about 7.5 billion hours watched per year from United States users.

Check

Once you get to an answer, spend some time quickly gut checking the value. Does it seem directionally accurate?

While the point of these question is not to get the answer exactly right, you are being evaluated on your problem solving skills and intuition. As such, demonstrate those one last time by validating your answer. If it seems right, great! And if it seems wrong, don't fret - that is simply an opportunity to talk through the assumptions you made which may have been incorrect. This will come across very well, and will *not* be interpreted negatively.

> **Candidate:** To quickly gut check this, let's compare it to TV. I think I've read before that the average amount of TV watched a day in the US is something like 3 hours, driven by a long tail of users who watch a *huge* amount of TV.
>
> Assuming that is correct, my Netflix average hours/day among users may be a little low. I may be underestimating how many people fall into the "binger" category of watching 10-20+ hours a week.
>
> **Interview**: Good intuition.

Hopefully this gives you a general idea of how to approach this type of question. If you want more practice, there are hundreds of resources out there to practice questions like this (sometimes called "Fermi Estimation Questions"). Remember that at end of the day, they are really all about structured thinking and communication.

As a final tip, always round the numbers to make the calculations easy. Don't waste too much time trying to do unnecessarily precise multiplications or divisions - you are not being evaluated on your ability to multiply weird values. Plus, it is all estimated anyways, so getting an exact value for any computation is nothing more than false precision. In the above question, the point where we said we would just round to 50 is a good example of how to do this.

Metrics and Analytics Questions

Being data-driven is absolutely *critical* to being an effective product manager. As part of every single product and feature you work on, you will be responsible for ensuring you have logged key events so that you can understand how people use your products. This is valuable on both a macro level ("How many daily active users do we have? What is our 5 week retention?"), and on a micro level ("What are the exact drop-off rates in our user sign-up funnel"). I should use these terms.

Quite simply, data is one of the best tools at a product manager's disposal. You will use data to help drive your product roadmap. You will use data to evaluate A/B tests and experiments you run in order to make the call on whether a new idea is actually good. And you will use data to help influence others and align the broader team, ensuring they understand how users are behaving and what that means for the product.

Because of this, companies interviewing product managers often ask metrics and analytics questions. These questions are a way for them to evaluate whether you will be a data driven (and therefore effective) PM. They want to ensure that you will:

1. Understand the key metrics that need to be measured for any given product
2. Understand the implications that certain metrics or data might have for a product
3. Understand how to run and evaluate A/B experiments

4. Understand how to *contextualize* data, and know when to go against the data (because data is imperfect)

There are entire books written about metrics and analytics (two we recommend are *Lean Analytics*[5] and *The Tyranny of Metrics*[6]). As such, a complete overview of how to think about metrics is well outside the scope of this book. That said, we can cover the basics, and give you a broad overview of how to think through, and prepare for, this type of PM interview question.

To start, let's dive into some key categories of analytics that tend to matter for most products:

[handwritten: 1. usage 2. retention & cohorts 3. engagement 4. funnels & sessions 5. experiments]

Usage

Often, the first thing someone thinks of when considering metrics is usage data - overall, how many people are using this product?

The most common way to measure usage is to look at something like daily-active-users ("DAUs") or monthly active users ("MAUs"). These are often the metrics people throw on dashboards, and are also often the metrics outlined in quarterly reports.

While usage metrics like this are a good way to quickly understand how popular a given product is, they are far from perfect, and you should be very careful to not over-rely on them.

[5] *Lean Analytics* by Alistair Croll and Benjamin Yoskovitz
[6] *The Tyranny of Metrics* by Jerry Muller

As an example, consider the following graph, which shows the daily active users for a product over the course of a few days. If this were your product, what could you conclude?

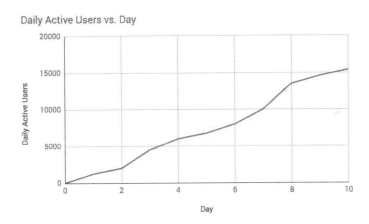

Daily Active Users vs. Day

You might say that it looks like the product is growing really quickly, and so it seems like people really like it!

The problem is that *just* looking at daily actives does not actually tell you if people are sticking with your product. What if it turned out that the data looks like the following once you split each day by *new* users vs *retained* users?

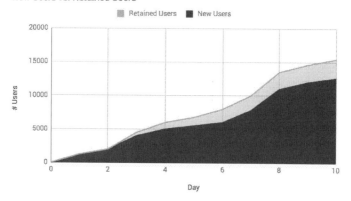

New Users vs. Retained Users

When you look at it this way, you can see that almost no users are staying with your product! They try it for one day, and then 90% or more never come back. While this might mean your marketing team is great, it also means your product is terrible!

A product manager who just looked at the first graph and thought things were good would be absolutely failing in their job.

This is why usage alone is basically never enough. It's a fine starting point and it's a number you should know, but you need to go further. The problem with usage metrics is that they are not generally directly actionable; they don't give much insight into the product you are designing.

So, in a PM analytics interview, it's great to start by highlighting the usage metrics you would look at, but quickly move on to the more interesting stuff.

define "active"

As a final point on usage, you want to be careful about how you define "active" if you are ever looking at usage metrics. Try to make the definition as close to the core value of your app if possible. Don't include people who simply visited your app or website for 5 seconds, did nothing, then left.

Retention and Cohorts

As we saw in the last example, retention is a much better way to understand whether people are sticking with your product. It's marketing's job to bring in new users, and it's your job to create a product that makes them want to stay!

There are countless ways to look at retention, but most of them ultimately boil down to looking at cohorts of users. A cohort of users is simply a group of users who started using the product at the same time. For instance - you might define a "Week 1" cohort who signed up for your product in the first week of the year.

The reason cohort analysis is valuable is because it involves looking at the same set of users over time. Of all the people who started using your product at time X, what happened to them over the next few days or weeks? It's probably some combination of:

1. People who stopped using the product completely
2. People who kept using the product consistently
3. People who quit, but then came back later

By engaging in this type of analysis, you can start to really understand the way users are reacting to your product and its features. You can differentiate marketing hype from product success.

A common way to visualize retention is to graph a grid of retention buckets:

Cohort	1 week	Retention N weeks later 2 weeks	3 weeks	4 weeks	5 weeks
Jan 1 - 8	50%	45%	40%	20%	20%
Jan 8 - 15	52%	50%	49%	30%	18%
Jan 15 - 22	51%	46%	40%	26%	25%
Jan 22 - 30	80%	67%	65%	60%	55%
Jan 31 - Feb 7	76%	72%	70%	60%	59%

This sample data shows what you might see if you launched a new feature focused on onboarding users the week of Jan 22 - 30. Ideally, such a feature would lead to a greater % of users being retained over time.

Engagement

Engagement is typically used to describe metrics which relate to the way users are interfacing with the product. For instance, Facebook News Feed engagement data would relate to the way users are doing things like posting to their feed, commenting on other posts, "poking" each other, reacting to other posts, and browsing through the news feed.

As a product manager, engagement metrics matter because they give direct insight into a few very important things:

1. **How do users actually use your product?**
2. **What are your user segments?**

3. How well designed are the features you have built?

Let's go through these one at a time.

First - engagement data gives you a way to understand how people actually use your product. For instance, going back to the Facebook News Feed example, it would be critical as a PM on News Feed to understand what the typical user behavior is for the product. This would involve asking questions like:

- What % of News Feed time is spent looking at posts by friends vs. ads?
- What is the typical length of a News Feed session? How long do users spend browsing?
- What is the distribution of different types of News Feed actions (likes, comments, etc) by users? Which are more and less common?
- How often do users hit a state where they hit the "end" of the feed, and need to wait for more content to load?

There are probably 10-20+ more questions in this vein you could ask about engagement. The reason it is absolutely essential to understand questions like this as a product manager is that the answers will fundamentally shape your priorities and product roadmap.

As a simple example, let's say the team could invest a few weeks doing some optimizations to heavily improve the rate that News Feed content loads.

A bad PM might say "Reduced latency sounds great. Let's do it!".

A good PM would first identify whether this is actually a problem for enough users by looking at the data. If only 5% of News Feed sessions involve a users hitting a loading state greater than 1 second, maybe this feature isn't actually worth building versus some of the other things you could do.

Understanding the data allows you to make these product tradeoffs, and to ensure you are always focusing on the highest impact work.

The second key use of engagement metrics is segmentation. No product has just one kind of user. As such, don't fall into the trap of always looking at averages or medians. Use data to help cluster your users into a few key categories or types. This will vastly improve the way you think about your product.

For example, let's consider Quora. I can almost guarantee that the distribution of questions asked per user looks something like the following: 95+% of users have never answered a question, and .1% of users probably provide 90+% of all answers.

If you were a Quora PM, understanding this breakdown would be absolutely critical, because it means you have *at least* two totally distinct, non-intersecting sets of users to consider. There is the "passive reader" segment, and the "power-answerer" segment. This would heavily shape how you think about building features for Quora.

For example, if you're building a feature that helps people answer questions, you better optimize it for the right .1% of your users. All your experiments and tests should be run on that set of users. Don't even worry about how it affects the rest, because they don't meaningfully contribute to answer content.

As another quick example, consider companies like Uber and Lyft. Do you think that users of these products tend to use either *only* the cheap options (e.g. Uber Pool) or *only* the luxury options (e.g. Uber Black)? Or, are there many users who utilize both the cheap and luxury options? The answer to this would change how you think about developing the product.

Almost any single time you get asked about analytics, it is worth considering your different user segments. Each segment will likely have its own target metrics, and its own key behavior you want to monitor.

The third key use of engagement metrics is to directly measure the impact of a specific feature you build. Any time you design a feature, you should consider the metrics that you will use to measure its success (or failure).

good vocab

In general, these metrics should not just be top line aggregate metrics (like overall product usage or customer satisfaction), but direct measurements of how the feature is impacting users within the product. The reason for this is that top line metrics tend to be lagging indicators of success and failure, and it's hard to directly attribute changes in them to individual features.

As an example, pretend you are the PM who launched Spotify's Discover Weekly playlist. Some of the engagement metrics you might look at for this feature would be:

1. **% of users who listen to discover weekly each week** - this shows how many people are generally aware of the feature and utilize it.

2. **Distribution of time spent listening to discover weekly each week by listeners (and comparing that vs. other content)** - this highlights how compelling the discover weekly content is.

3. **% of listened to discover weekly songs marked as "love", "hate", and not voted on** - this identifies how good the recommendation engine is.

Let's say not very many people are listening, but you see really high time spent and lots of "love" ratings by those who do. This might indicate that you're not doing enough to help market or promote the playlist to users. You may want to work on refining the different discovery points into the playlist within the product.

In contrast, let's say you see a large % of users using discover weekly, and a large amount of time spent listening, but high "hate" ratings. This might mean people are giving it a chance now because it is new or they like the idea, but they aren't actually liking the recommendations. In that case, you better devote all your time to improving the recommendation algorithm before these users give up on the feature.

As a final tip, make sure you are normalizing your engagement numbers. For instance, assume you launch a new "Made by Amazon" product on Amazon. A naive thought would be to simply track overall sales. But, what if the product category grows a lot, while at the same time your product's share within that category lowers? Technically, your sales would be going up, but your product itself would nonetheless be losing out to competitors. Tracking sales *relative* to the category would be a better metric.

Funnels and Sessions

One other really common way to look at product usage data is funnels. Basically, this is just the series of drop-off rates at each step in a multi-step process.

For example, one key funnel for Amazon.com would probably be:

1. User views product page
2. User adds product to cart
3. User visits cart
4. User says they want to checkout
5. User enters billing/shipping info
6. User confirms the order

You can be sure that every single change to Amazon's e-commerce website is being evaluated against this funnel of actions. A change to the billing flow, for instance, better improve the % of users who go from billing to order confirmation.

More broadly, funnels are just a way of thinking about user sessions, or a series of subsequent actions by a user. Many product questions require you to look at things in this way, rather than just evaluating isolated user actions.

Experiments

Finally, you should know the basic principles of experiments. An experiment (or A/B test) is simply a situation where you take a new feature, and selectively launch it to only a random subset of all users. You then compare metrics between the set of users with new feature (the *experimental* group), and the set of users without it (the *control* group).

What is the purpose of this?

Let's say you launch a new layout for the Google search results page which you expect will improve users' click-through-rate. You decide to launch this normally, without an experiment. You look at the metrics, and see that the overall click-through-rate is up in the week since the feature launched. Sounds great, right?

Well, maybe. The problem is that you can not directly conclude that the change in the data was due to your feature. For example, what if:

1. A big international event got a lot of attention, changing the types of queries people type. Those queries may have better click-through-rates in general.
2. A big marketing push led people to change the types of queries they type into google search this week.
3. Another feature launched this week which improved click through rate.

Basically, there are tens to hundreds of other variables that might have impacted the click-through-rate. It's quite possible your change actually *reduced* the click through rate, but one of these other variables counteracted that and made the overall click-through-rate higher.

Be able to explain why A/B tests are generally a good idea.

The way to get around this is by running an experiment. If set-up properly, because you are *randomly* assigning users between the control and experimental groups, the experiment evens out all variables except the one you want to look at - your feature. Everything should be the same between the two groups *except* your feature, which means any difference in metrics between the groups is due to your feature. This lets you evaluate it in an unbiased manner.

Experiments are extremely common in tech companies for this reason, and as a PM you will likely run them very often.

—

At this point, we've given you a baseline understanding of some of the key types of metrics, and how to use each. Now, let's put your newfound knowledge to the test! Consider the following interview question:

"Let's say you are the product manager for a new Airbnb Plus program, where Airbnb hosts who meet certain extra criterion can get listed as 'Airbnb Plus' hosts to users, and get a higher share of the booking revenue for each booking. What metrics would you look at to analyze the success of this program?"

One last time, take 10-15 minutes to try to answer this yourself. Push yourself to think as broadly as possible - what are all the different facets of such a program, and how would you measure each?

Done?

Alright, here is how we would answer it:

Interviewer: Let's say you are the product manager for a new Airbnb Plus program, where Airbnb hosts who meet certain extra criterion get listed as "Airbnb Plus" hosts to users, and get a higher share of the booking revenue for each booking. What metrics would you look at to analyze the success of this program?

Candidate: Can you give me a few minutes to think through this?

Interviewer: Sure (2 minutes pass)

Candidate: Okay, so to start, I think it's helpful to define the key aspects and goals of a program like this. From there, we can determine the right metrics to measure each piece.

At a high level, I would break down the program into the following elements:

- The process for a host to become part of Airbnb Plus
- The experience of a user browsing Airbnb and viewing Airbnb Plus branded homes
- The experience of a user who stays in Airbnb Plus branded homes
- The experience of a host after they become part of Airbnb Plus

To help determine the right metrics to look at for each piece, I would start by considering the goals for each of these elements.

First, let's talk through the process to become an Airbnb Plus host. Do you know to what extent this process is host driven vs.

Airbnb driven? (e.g. Airbnb reaches out to a select few hosts, or there is some form of application process)

Interviewer: Let's say its Airbnb driven

Candidate: In that case, I would assume Airbnb might have the following goals:

1. Reach out to the highest quality hosts to ensure these experiences are excellent for users
2. Ensure hosts opt-in to the program at a high rate
3. Keep the program selective/prestigious (if too many hosts were part of Airbnb Plus, it would no longer have any signaling value)

So, how would I quantify these things? For #1, I would look at data like the hosts' ratings, # of stays, # of reviews, the labels that users can assign to a home (e.g. "Cozy"), the number of times Airbnb has had to intervene for stays on the hosts' homes, and maybe some sort of aggregate analysis on the comments for their homes. On all these factors, you would likely want to start only with hosts at the 90th percentile and above.

I would want to use this criteria to determine who Airbnb should reach out to, and I would also want to track it over time, perhaps ensuring that no Airbnb Plus host eventually drops beneath certain thresholds.

Especially in the early days, this would be important because users have to feel like there is a clear "step up" in value by staying in a home branded this way. Otherwise, there won't be any user trust in the program.

I would measure #2 (host opt-in) primarily by looking at the funnel of steps it takes for a host to be confirmed. While I do not know the full details of the program, I imagine there may be a series of steps such as

- Airbnb reaches out
- Host confirms interest
- Host has to verify/prove a few things about their home
- Host has to sign some sort of final statement committing themselves to do certain things moving forwards

I would want to understand where in this funnel you see large drop-offs. For instance, let's say there is a very poor response rate after Airbnb reaches out. In that case, we may want to experiment with alternative ways of pitching or positioning the feature, to make it more enticing. Or, we may want to change the way the host is alerted of the benefits (email vs. in product, etc).

For #3 (keeping the program selective), I would just want to measure, at any given time, what % of hosts are part of the program. We likely want to ensure it stays somewhat selective, so that Airbnb Plus does not just become the "default".

Okay, so that covers the key things I would measure to help assess the process to become part of Airbnb Plus. Before I move on, any questions about what I just said?

Interviewer: Nope, feel free to continue.

Candidate: Great. So, the next area I mentioned was the user experience of browsing Airbnb if such a program exists. I assume that Airbnb Plus homes would be marked/designated in some way, and I assume the goal of this is to make such homes more enticing to users by creating more trust, since the user knows that this home meets certain standards.

Given that, the key metrics I would look at are the ways that users are engaging with Airbnb Plus listed homes vs. traditional homes within the Airbnb product. For example:

- What is the click-through-rate of Airbnb Plus listed homes on the Airbnb search UI vs. other homes?
- What % of the time do users actively filter for Airbnb Plus homes while searching
- What is the booking request rate of people who view an Airbnb Plus listed home vs. other homes?

For a lot of this, you would probably want to run some experiments. For instance, take the same home listing, and for some % of users, show the "Airbnb Plus" badge, but don't for others. Then, amongst those groups, compare these click through and booking rates. This would help you much more directly quantify if the badging has an impact on user's booking decisions.

Interviewer: Let's say there was *not* a difference in those rates for such an experiment. Would that mean this program is a failure?

Candidate: Not necessarily. It's possible that this program only starts to meaningfully make an impact on users once they have stayed in one of these homes. Once they do, they see what a difference the program makes, and as a result have a strong preference to stay again at such places in the future. I think that would still be positive result overall - it just means that the badging alone doesn't have a big impact on users.

I think there are two ways to evaluate this point. One would be to look at the same metrics I mentioned above, but only among users who already stayed in Airbnb Plus at least once. The second would be to analyze how ratings + reviews trend for Airbnb Plus homes - are they dramatically better than other homes?

These are actually some of the key metrics I would have mentioned for the third element - the user experience at an Airbnb Plus home. You would expect users to enjoy it much more than normal, and so would therefore hope to see higher interest in similar homes in the future, as well as better than average ratings and reviews.

Interviewer: Makes sense

Candidate: Finally, the last piece we haven't touched on is the experience of hosts in the program. I imagine the key goals here are that hosts see value in the program, remain part of it, and perhaps even become more active as a result of it. So, I would probably want to look at things like: user satisfaction with the program via surveys, host retention in the program, and the change in a host's activity and engagement with users on Airbnb after joining the program.

If there is indeed a monetary incentive for hosts to be in Airbnb Plus (e.g. higher share of revenues), I would probably also want to quantify exactly the difference hosts end up getting. This could end up being an effective sales tactic for future hosts to join the program (e.g. "Airbnb Plus homes tend to make 25+% more"). I might also look at if there is a change in utilization of the homes for hosts in Airbnb Plus (e.g. home booked 90+% of the time vs. 60% of the time), as that would be another compelling sells point for hosts to join.

The above answer demonstrates a few key things to keep in mind when answering about metrics.

First, you should always be tying metrics to product goals. As a PM, your job first and foremost is to build a successful product. As such, you want to really dig into what will help you do that. The answer above very clearly highlighted what the different goals of this feature might be, and then discussed ways to quantify or measure each of those goals (or to quantify information which would help in the pursuit of those goals).

Second, notice how we clearly explained why each metric is worthwhile. We didn't just list every possible thing we could measure. We were very precise about the purpose of each metric.

Third, notice how we, as always, maintained a very clear and easy to follow structure. We broke the problem down into pieces, and then discussed each piece one by one, asking for feedback at each step as we could. Don't forgot to do this!

Finally, note how product ideas were worked into the answer, and how we sometimes discussed what we might do as a PM if we saw certain trends in the data. This is crucial and helps elevate your answer. It shows you not only understand *what* to measure, but also *how* to interpret and utilize that information.

Technical Interviews

You may notice that we did not call out technical interviews as one of the primary types of interviews you will have as a product manager. There's a reason for this - only a couple of companies will give new grad product managers coding or technical interviews.

Google is notorious for giving APM candidates one technical interview when you go on-site. However, other companies such as Facebook and Uber do not give technical interviews to new grad product managers. As such, whether or not you should actively prepare for this will depend a little bit on which companies you are applying to.

If you know a company you are interested in gives technical interviews, how should you prepare? Well, let's start with what you shouldn't do - endless algorithm practice on Leetcode. In general, PM technical interviews are not like software engineering interviews. You won't get asked really detailed coding questions as a PM.

What will you get asked about? Google (and similar companies) mostly wants to make sure you will be able to work with engineers. They want to know:

1. Can the candidate communicate with engineers and understand what they mean?

2. Can the candidate talk through all the components and systems that would need to be built in order to support a given product design or product vision? Do they

understand the engineering implications of a product decision?

3. Can the candidate consider engineering trade offs when making product decisions? Can they reason about how making a certain engineering decision will impact the product?

You'll note that none of this involves writing down a dynamic programming algorithm. Rather, you will be asked higher-level system design questions, and be probed on your ability to think through the engineering side of product decisions (and the product side of engineering decisions).

Here are some rough examples of what we mean:

1. Walk me through how ordering a Lyft works. Outline the high-level system components and how they would interact. List 5 key trade-offs the team likely had to make when designing this system, and their impact on the product.

2. You're working on a flight search product, and from UX research you have learned that your search loading takes far too long, and you're losing a lot of customers as a result. Talk me through ideas for how to reduce flight search latency.

3. You're launching XYZ product. What metrics would you look at? What would be a possible database schema for those metrics? How would you query for Z metric?

4. Consider app X. Let's say a designer wants to make Y change to Z user flow. What are the most important engineering considerations for this change? What would need to be changed to make this happen? Can you roughly estimate the complexity of that change?

Hopefully, this gives you a somewhat clear sense of the type of questions you will be asked in a technical interview (and, honestly, this is the type of thinking you will need to do as a PM as well).

If you followed our advice earlier in this book on ensuring that you have the right technical background, these questions should not be a big issue for you. Here are a few pieces of advice to help you prepare:

1. Review basic data structures and algorithms. You don't need to be an expert and we can almost guarantee you won't be asked to implement a sorting algorithm. But, the baseline knowledge is useful context.

2. Review the core terminology and concepts often involved in technical systems. E.g. databases, caching, client vs. server logic, APIs and API design, threads,

etc. Basically, all the things taught in Computer Architecture and Operating Systems classes.

3. Do system design practice questions. A few books and websites cover this sort of thing (e.g. *Cracking the Coding Interview*[7]). You can also just take apps or products you like to use, and spend 30 minutes mapping out how they work on a whiteboard. Have a friend critique what you missed or overlooked.

With all of that said, don't worry *too much* about technical interviews when applying for new grad PM roles. The technical interview is about hitting a certain threshold: is there a high likelihood you can work well with an engineering team?

Get the basics down, and then focus on the other types of interviews you will have, where there is a much greater opportunity (and need) to hit the ball out of the park. You can certainly get knocked out of the process for doing poorly in your technical interview, but you won't get hired unless you crush the product interviews.

The One Question to Prepare For

We've mentioned a few times that it is very hard to predict what companies or products you may be asked about in a PM interview. This is why most of our interview discussions so far have centered around *how* to answer PM questions.

---

[7] *Cracking the Coding Interview* by Gayle Laakmann McDowell

However, there is one question where it is worth it to have an answer ready in your back pocket. This question generally looks like:

> **Interviewer**: List a 1-3 products you've been using a lot recently or are really passionate about.

> **Candidate**: I really like to use X, Y, and Z.

> **Interview**: Okay, let's assume that you are the head of product for Z. I want you to walk me through, end to end, what the next feature they should build is, how you would build it, and how you would launch it.

Many PM interviewers like to ask you for a product or company that you can speak in depth about. From there, they will typically probe you on all aspects of that company, covering strategy, product design, analytics, and more.

We highly recommend having 3 go-to companies or products which you are ready to talk about in depth. Write out a full analysis of each one before your interviews. Be ready to talk about competitors, target users, current pain points, market trends, and more. In other words, pretend you are the CEO or head of product for that company.

Believe us, if you end up getting asked this question, you'll be very glad you did this.

How to Practice

At some level, practicing for PM interviews is fairly straightforward. At this point, you know what kinds of questions you will be asked and you know the characteristics you need to demonstrate in your responses, such as structured analytical thinking, clear communication, product insight and creativity. The only thing left to do is practice!

What we mean by this is that you should find some time every day, or a at least a couple of times a week, where you can spend just 5-10 minutes developing your PM interview skills. This might be a morning shower or an evening commute; all that matters is that you have a small amount of time where you can speak out loud to yourself.

During these time periods, pretend you are answering a PM interview question. Think of some company, product, or app that have been using or read about recently, and come up with a question about it. For instance:

1. What is the board of directors thinking?

2. What is the biggest strategic or competitive risk?

3. Design a feature for it

4. Estimate something about it

5. Identify the metrics you would look at as the product owner

6. What are the 3 three biggest issues with the current product design?

You get the idea. From there, practice answering the question you came up with verbally. Speaking will force you to consider communication structure in a way that thinking doesn't - it is much harder to articulate and organize your thoughts when you are talking out loud. You also want to make sure you are answering as if you were in an interview. Pretend you are speaking to someone who cannot see into your mind - you want to make sure that *anyone*, even your mom or dad, could follow your line of reasoning.

Your answer doesn't have to be comprehensive or perfect - your goal is simply to get into the PM interview mindset on a regular basis. If you do this for a couple of weeks, you will dramatically improve at PM interviews. You will have trained yourself to think like a product manager, which at the end of the day is what your interviewers are looking for.

Our second key piece of advice for practicing is to get someone else to ask you practice questions. A friend or acquaintance who listens to you will be able to identify situations where your logic isn't clear, your analyses don't make sense, or your communication is weak. It will be hard to duplicate this type of feedback on your own.

Ideally, this would be someone who works, or has worked, in product management or the tech industry. However, if you don't know anyone like this, don't fret. **Having anyone at all interview you is still exceptionally useful**. In fact, having someone who knows *nothing* about technology can in many cases be uniquely beneficial.

Being interviewed by someone with no tech background will force you to be crystal clear in your communication and reasoning so that *even they can understand you*. If you can give an end-to-end product analysis of Uber, and you can do it in a such a simple and straightforward way that even your parents could understand you, you will excel at PM interviews.

Don't discredit feedback from this type of interviewer with the line of thinking that "Oh, someone who was actually interviewing me would have understood what I meant". Instead, if they mention that they didn't fully understand something, force yourself to explain it better. Make your analysis so structured and your communication so clear that they can follow every word you say.

When having someone interview you, you can either give them a question to ask you, or you can ask them to come up with one. The benefit of the latter approach is it will better mirror the surprise of a real interview. The good news is that it is pretty easy to train someone how to come up with a PM interview question. Just have them pick some company or product and ask you a question about it. If the interviewer is non-technical, you can also make it a bit easier for them by instructing them to specifically ask you about a non-tech product (for instance - "How would you improve a refrigerator").

If you practice the PM interview regularly on your own, as well as go through full practice questions with friends, family, or acquaintances a couple of times, you will be very well prepared for PM interviews.

In terms of timeline, we would recommend starting to actively prepare at least a month before any interview you have. During this time, strive to think a little bit about products and companies every day, and go through at least 4-5 full practice questions with other people.

Other Resources for PM Interviews

We've now given you a whirlwind tour of PM interviews, highlighting the best ways to prepare and the key types of questions you may get asked.

That said, a full guide for mastering PM interviewing is outside the scope of this book.

As such, if you want to see more fully worked out practice questions and problems, we highly recommend the following two books: *Cracking the PM Interview* by Gayle Laakmann McDowell and *Decode and Conquer* by Lewis Lin. Each is filled with tens to hundreds of sample PM interview questions. These books are a great way to take your interview preparation to the next level.

We also recommend the following online resources for PM interviews:

- www.productmanagerhq.com
- www.pmlesson.com
- www.thepminterview.com

Chapter 15

Comparing Offers

Hopefully, you've used everything we've taught you to apply, interview for, and land an offer or two as a new grad product manager! In this chapter, we'll highlight strategies for choosing between offers. These are the criteria you should likely be considering when making a decision on where to work out of college as a new grad PM.

Product

This should be obvious! Your job as a product manager is to be the owner of a product and drive it forward, so you better like the product you work on. If you aren't excited by it, you almost certainly will not reach your full potential as a PM, since so much of being a good product manager is about being a power user of your own product.

So, ask yourself: what type of product do you want to work on? Would you rather work on something consumer-facing or developer facing? Do you have a specific interest area, such as social networks or transportation? Do ecosystems fascinate you? Would you rather work on APIs than on products with user interfaces?

These questions can help guide you into making the right decision. For example, if you're considering offers from Facebook and Uber and you aren't very excited by social networks, we would highly recommend not choosing Facebook. There is too high a probability you will end up on a product that doesn't mean anything to you.

Note that the type of product you work on will also end up affecting your role and job responsibilities as a PM. If you work on developer-facing APIs, you may almost *never* work with designers. In contrast, if you work on the consumer-facing side of a social network, you'll work with designers all the time. If you work on an enterprise product, you'll likely interface a lot with sales and customer support. That will be less true if you work on a product that targets small businesses.

As such, you should not only consider the products that excite you but the working style that excites you. For instance, if you like being technical and UI design annoys you, then find a company where the PM job will be more slanted towards technical and backend work.

What makes this a bit more challenging as a new grad PM is that you often have a blanket offer from a company, not an offer from a specific team within that company. Furthermore, many new grad PM programs involve rotations, meaning you will need to switch roles at least a couple of times in your first few years.

As such, you need to look at the companies holistically. How broad is their product range? What are their areas of focus? What percentage of their products would you like to work on? A basic analysis here can give you a pretty good idea of which companies are good fits for you, and which aren't.

Culture

Culture is likely the most important thing to consider after product. Different companies have very different working environments, and it's critical that you find one that suits your personality. Otherwise, you're likely to be both unhappy and ineffective.

To evaluate a company's culture, meet as many people who work there as you can. Try to understand what the company values, and how people within the company work together. It can be helpful to ask the people you meet what they like and don't like about working there.

Some of the things you may want to consider include:

- Is it a collaborative environment, or a more competitive one?
- Is it a sales-driven company, or a more engineering driven one?
- Do people spend time together outside of work?
- Do the company's social functions revolve around drinking, or around board games?
- What types of employees does the company try to hire?
- What are the company's values?
- How flexible is the working environment?

Note that the size of a company can also dramatically influence the culture and working style.

Larger companies like Google and Facebook have the advantage of giving you lots of structure. Even if you are working on a relatively new area within Google, you'll have plenty of opportunities to be mentored and to leverage all of the internal resources Google has to offer. Another benefit of working at a large company is that many products are already used by hundreds of millions or even billions of users. There's a really surreal feeling to launching a product on Google Search and knowing that billions of people will immediately start using it.

On the other hand, there's an electric feeling to working in a smaller environment with a close-knit team. But, startups can be chaotic, and there is a lot less hand-holding. You'll probably also have to work a lot more hours.

By figuring out the cultural characteristics and working environment that sits well with you, it will be a lot easier to choose between offers.

People

While you were interviewing, did you get a sense of the people that worked at the company? Were they people that motivated you and inspired you?

Surrounding yourself with great people who you would like to work with is so important. If possible, try to at least meet your manager. There are few things that matter as much to your job satisfaction as your manager. Ask yourself - is this someone that wants to help you grow? Is this someone you can learn from?

If you're able to meet your broader team, that's even better. As a product manager, you will be interacting with people from multiple departments and disciplines, so knowing who your key counterparties will be in engineering, design, business development, and more can give you a lot of useful information.

If you find a company with the right product, culture, and people, you're basically guaranteed to love your job. And if you love your job, you will be able to perform really well.

From the Insiders - First Year Google APM

"Working as a PM at Google is an incredible experience. You are constantly challenged by some of the toughest problems out there while being supported by really bright people. It has been a place where I can develop both as a creator and a leader.

Culturally, Google hires for very nice, friendly, and supportive people. I really appreciate the working environment that comes from that. Google is also very transparent and bottoms up, which allows me to see the broader vision for the company and provides me more ownership in my role.

Google also has such a large range of products - hardware, consumer products, developers tools, healthcare initiatives, moonshot bets, and so much more. I feel like I could never get bored working here."

From the Insiders - First Year Linkedin APM

"During my recruitment process, I mainly considered product management opportunities at tech companies with established programs. I also spent some time exploring PM opportunities at startups, as well as some software engineering roles. Ultimately, I decided that I'd receive the best training and resources at a tech company with an established APM program. I interviewed with a bunch of companies and eventually chose LinkedIn.

The things that stood out to me about LinkedIn were: the company's emphasis on talent development, the size of the product team (LinkedIn is under 200 PMs, compared to over 1000 at Google), tremendous access to mentors, and ample opportunity to work on side projects outside of work."

Conclusion

We remember when we were in college and first heard about the Google APM program - we wanted to be part of it, but we didn't really know what to do to get there. There were hardly any resources out there about how to apply or what interviews were like, and there weren't many people to reach out to either. Furthermore, while the job vaguely sounded amazing, we didn't *truly* understand what it was actually like. This book represents all the resources and knowledge we wish we had back then.

Each year, companies like Google and Facebook hire only *tens* of product managers out of college, compared to thousands of software engineers. Becoming a product manager out of college is *tough*, and you'll be competing against some absurdly smart and impressive people (believe us - we're constantly amazed by the other new grad PMs we've met in our programs).

We wanted to give you a leg up in this process; to walk you through the ins and outs of becoming a PM. We hope you have gained a strong understanding of how to position yourself to get one of these jobs. We also hope you better understand what it is like to work as a product manager and whether or not you would be a good fit.

Being a product manager is a unique and exciting opportunity, but as we've explained, it also has its challenges and downsides. Our goal with this book wasn't really to sell you on product management so much as distill exactly what the job is like so that you can make an informed decision. So, whether this book helped you decide to take your first step towards product management, or has convinced you it is not the right career move at all, we hope you learned something. If you are in the former category, we wish you the best of luck in becoming a product manager.

If you have questions for us, or want to send us feedback about the book, check out www.collegeproductmanager.com.

-Davis and Alan

Made in the USA
Middletown, DE
19 March 2019